Senior Cares

Jessica Solomon

ISBN:147817059X
ISBN-13:9781478170594

DEDICATION

For Pa. There will always be a special place in my heart for you.
Tell Joe Chicken Newts and Reuben Noodleman I said, "Hello".
We still miss you.

CONTENTS

ACKNOWLEDGMENTS

I would like to thank my mother and father for all their pearls of wisdom. I would like to share my appreciation for all the people in senior care that are truly committed to serving others. I am blessed that I had the opportunity to work in the senior care industry. I have had many blessings and made friendships that will last a lifetime.

CHAPTER ONE - I LOVE OLD PEOPLE?

Whatever profession you are in or whatever you may be doing for your main source of income, do you ever wonder if the rest of the world gives thought to that industry or profession? Most people (that I know) have vehicles. At one time or another you have to have your vehicle serviced for one reason or another. I am not sure if the mechanic, technician, or car wash guy is giving thought to what he does every day and how his profession affects their community, family or other families. What their thoughts and feelings of their everyday profession is a mystery to me. I only really have firsthand thoughts and feelings about what I do and I would like to uncover some mystery about that Industry and things most people would never think of and quite honestly would never know some of the truth otherwise.

I'm an old soul. I have been told this a ton of times. Not that I needed the memo, because when you are an old soul you just know you are. I always migrated towards adults when I was young. I was the little entertainer and very bold to say the least. You can ask my mother's best friend, Sheila. She knows. Shelia has been my mother's best friend for over 50 years. Shelia loves to tell people when I was about four or five out of nowhere I asked her, "Shelia, are you a virgin?"

Shelia has had several volunteer positions over the years. She volunteered at a local hospital and had several positions where she was assisting old people.

My mother, Nancy, would say, "Shelia just loves old people".

What is that all about? She loves old people?

I asked my mother, "What do you mean she loves old people? Why does she love old people?"

Nancy said, "I don't know. Shelia just does. She thinks they are cute. She likes to help them".

I had to sit on that one. Do I love old people? I never really thought about it. I know I always migrated to older people. That is, people that are older than me. When I was in elementary school and all the kids were on the playground I stayed close to the teachers that stood in a group monitoring all the kids. They would try to encourage me to play with the other kids. I found that their conversations were so much more stimulating. Plus, I was a real charming and witty kid. I could make anyone laugh and I do love a good audience.

In fifth grade I spent half my time floating around the school. I would spend most days passing notes from my teacher, Mr. Davente to Mrs. Agosini all the way at the other end of the school. My teacher would write a note, fold it, staple it and then hand it to me. I would take the note and bring it to Mrs. Agosini. She would open it and then have a chuckle and then reply to it and then fold it, staple it, and hand back to me. I would then return the note to Mr. Davente. You get the picture, it went on all day. Some days I would spend hours in Mrs. Agosini's class and just review her class's tests and grade papers. One day all the kids in my fifth grade class was up in arms about this and demanded to know why I was excused from reading assignments in class and didn't have to take some of the tests like the rest of them. It was a real mutiny on the bounty.

My family moved from Long Island after fifth grade. I got an autograph book at the end of fifth grade which you would typically do after the end of sixth grade, but I knew I wouldn't be returning. Mr. Davente wrote in my book, "Jessica, I hope you learned as much as you taught me."

When I was in summer camp I much preferred hanging with the camp counselors. They loved me, too. I often found myself wandering campus bopping around from one counselor to the other. I rarely participated in my group's gatherings. I seriously was M.I.A. from most group activities, but I seemed to go about my day being pretty independent and never did find a specific group I connected with other than the counselors.

Once I was walking along a path by myself that led me to a face to face encounter with the camp owner, Marty. It was just he and I and it was my big moment to address a much needed subject that was an ongoing issue at the camp. I felt compelled to reveal an unjust conspiracy that had been the subject of a lot of attention that summer. It was something that did not settle well with me. That's just me. I like rooting for the underdog. I like to see justice prevail.

I walked up to Marty and I said, "I have something I have to tell you. Behind your back the kids call you Marty Farty".

Marty Farty patted me on the head and gave me a reassuring smile. He said, "I know".

It really wasn't the reaction I thought I would get. I am not sure what I was expecting. I mean really, was I looking for a reward or some other type of recognition? My point is that I felt compelled to share the truth. I don't like the shadiness of unjust gossip and rumors. Like is there really a just reason for gossip and rumors? Of course, I get to determine that. I don't like being made a fool of and I don't like when others are made a fool when it is not

3

deserved. Again, I make those determinations as well. I think the truth shall set you free and it's always good to help others when you think they can use a helping hand. Apparently, at the time I thought I was doing Marty a favor.

Another example of me migrating towards older peeps was my decision to attend college a year early. I did early admissions at the local community college and then I commuted to a university to complete my bachelor's degree in Science. The university I attended didn't exactly cater to the sciences. That university was more about arts and theater. So the other students that shared my major were mainly commuters like me. The majority of students were older than me. Some were ten to twenty years older. So there again, I find myself hanging, studying and socializing with a much older crowd.

I never had experience with much older or old people. The only really old folks that I knew were my grandparents, my mother's parents, Ma and Pa. I had a few great aunts and great uncles on my mother's side as well. Pa was a great grandfather. He was a man that wore his heart on his sleeve. He adored his grandchildren. Pa had six granddaughters. He was sweet and funny and he liked to talk and have conversations. He would make up stories about imaginary characters like Joe Chicken-newts and Ruben Noodleman. Joe Chicken-newts was actually a real guy. Ruben Noodleman? Pa would draw pictures of him, but Ruben would always be hiding behind a fence.

Many years after Pa had died I was hanging with my cousin Jaime. We were out partying and she told me that years ago she asked, "Pa, I really want to see a picture of Ruben Noodleman and Joe Chicken-newts." Pa said, "Jaime, I don't think I have any pictures, but I may have the negatives". He proceeded to give

Jaime negatives of photos which she intently studied to get a glimpse of these men of mystery. At the time she told me the story we both looked at each other and it was at that moment I think she realized that Pa was being a prankster. Something you don't think of when you are a kid. Pa was probably really proud of himself for that one.

Ma, unlike Pa, was not super bubbly and not the warmest grandma in the world. I think she loved us grandchildren and we loved her, she just had an odd way of showing it. I would get so excited when my grandparents came for a visit. I would run home from school that day. I was so excited to see them. Pa always gave wet kisses and tight hugs. Ma would give you a big hug, then she would put her hands on your face and squeeze it and say, "Oh, I love you Bubbie", and then she would shove your face to the side and say, "now go away!" It was very odd, but that was just her way. I remember forewarning any of my friends before they came for a visit if my grandmother was around. I just thought a brief explanation of her actions was needed. It was like a "just in case my grandmother does this or that" kind of thing. I didn't want my friends to be scarred in any way.

So, there was really my only experience with "old people". Of course, there was also Ma's sister, Aunt Libby a.k.a. the Incredible Shrinking Woman. She was super sweet. She was the opposite of Ma. Also, Ma and Pa always bickered. Once, my cousin, Rachel, pretended like she was a reporter during the Olympics. Rachel was interviewing my grandparents about their thoughts about the events on TV. Something snapped in one of my grandparents and they went into a typical full blown argument. They continued to argue in front of my cousins Jaime and Rachel like they weren't even there. Rachel turned her recording session about the

Olympics into a reporting session much like a boxing main event and stated that she was currently at "The Ma and Pa wars". It's true. We have it on tape.

So, do I love old people? I know I loved my grandparents very much. I know I loved my grandmother despite of her flaws and hurtful ways. I appreciated her the time I visited her in Florida and she encouraged me to spend my money on a bracelet I desperately wanted, but I didn't want to part with my cash. Ma said, "Jessica, sometimes you just have to treat yourself." That stuck with me. Those are some of the things you remember.

I also remember the only time my grandfather was annoyed with me. We were sitting on the front stoop at my family's house in Upstate, New York. I was stomping on some ants and Pa gave me that "what did that ant ever do to you?" speech. That stuck with me, too. To this day I will rarely ever harm a spider. I will pick it up with a tissue and toss it outside. Pa was a real lover of animals. After Pa gave me that speech, he proceeded to tell me that he wanted me to know how much he cared about me. Pa said, "Jessica, there will always be a special place in my heart for you." My grandfather was actively dying at the time. I didn't know that, but he did.

I know Pa was a wonderful man and many people genuinely liked him. He suffered an agonizing and unfair death and he was taken from us too soon. When we reminisce about Pa it is generally uplifting stories. Heartfelt and funny, just like Pa. I never thought about whether or not I had a love or passion for old people. I loved Pa and we all still miss him very much.

CHAPTER 2 -SALES OR BUST

When I was a little girl I didn't imagine walking down an aisle with a white wedding dress, getting married and having kids. It just wasn't something I really considered. As a matter of fact, in third grade we created books that were "All about me". It took you through each decade of my life and future predictions of what I thought my life would be like. In my twenties I thought I would be a rock star. I think I was a lawyer in my forties. In my eighties I thought I would be in a rocking chair, listening to a radio and having my nieces and nephews at my feet. Anybody notice that throughout the years I had some pretty fabulous careers and never mentioned my future husband or children?

I have had many jobs. Like most people I had retail and food service jobs before and during college. I was really good at retail and being a sales associate. Even if the only recognition was my name on a board with stars I would strive to get the highest average sell. I was queen of Up Selling. And if you tied some commission to the competition I would nail it out of the ball park. I have a way of convincing the purchaser that they couldn't afford NOT to buy the upgraded combo meal or whatever it was that I was selling.....cookies, jewelry, clothes, cocktails, whatever. My selling technique is better than average. I can only sell something if I believe in my product or service. If I don't believe in it, then my better than average selling technique cannot be applied and therefore, I lose the ability to sell well.

So, here I am this great salesperson and when I go to college I major in Science. I hate to put the blame on someone, but the reality is I really didn't know what I wanted to major in and the other truth is my father made me major in science. I had to. It was the deal we made. It was a ticket to a new car, independence, skipping twelfth grade and one year closer to moving to California. I figured that I'd somehow figure it all out later.

When I came to CA I took the first job I could get. It paid six dollars an hour to do data entry at a medical research center. I had to go through stacks of clippings of obituaries and remove the names of the deceased from our mailing list. It was a temporary position that was only to last about three months. About two weeks into the job the staff members realized that I would probably be done with the project in less than a month in a half. Always late, I would rush to work to make sure I was on time or within three minutes of my scheduled time. I have no idea why I put so much pressure on myself. I would watch in amazement on how most employees would stroll in and out of work. By ten a.m. half of them had been on twenty breaks and smoked five cigarettes and drank 5 coffees.

I sat in the front office with a gal that was probably in her late fifties. Her name was Jeanine. One day Jeanine said, "You know, we just love east coasters. East coasters work so fast and get the job done so quickly."

I looked at Jeanine and said with all seriousness, "You know, in New York if you don't work, they FIRE you." I'll just add that to my long list of reasons that I am so glad I grew up in New York. I figured out very quickly that this would be a town to easily shine in. There wasn't much competition for hard workers in this state. It's not better or worse out here in CA. It's just different, a little more laid back –to say the least.

So, I proceeded on in careers. I worked as an admin in the

Quality Assurance and Regulatory Compliance departments at a raw material manufacturer. It's there that I realized my true calling and that I was just born to do sales and I should pursue a career in that field. There was clearly no opportunity for a sales position at that company so I migrated to a medical device manufacturer. I worked in the Clinical Research department. Their main product was breast implants. I figured I'd have a shot to get into other departments and eventually into sales if I did my time. Boy, did I do my time all right in "tit city". That place was like a prison to me. More like a Chinese torture cell. I hated that job and after a year and a half I found myself at a Telecommunications company.

The telecommunications company was a good gig. It wasn't ultimately what I wanted to do, but it was a professional job that was teaching me more skills and would ultimately bring me closer to my career goals. I was in a customer support position in a highly technical field and I was able to manage accounts and support outside sale representatives. I really embraced my role and was very diligent with my responsibilities.

There were two managers in the customer support division and they were a total yin and yang. My hiring manager had way more people skills and understood the dynamics of human resources and managed her people with a real nurturing attitude. The other manager had a real technical background and understood the business inside and out which was in some ways mastering a language like Japanese to me. I knew what the technical manager thought of me. I could hear her thoughts about me through telepathy. She did not make much of an effort to speak to me or even acknowledge me at first. I knew that she never would have considered hiring me. Sooner or later, I won her over and she transitioned me to her team which was the most advanced and experienced support team in the company.

Three and a half years passed. The time paid off and I was given the opportunity to work in a more sales support/inside sales role. Unfortunately, the company closed its local doors. I had the opportunity to continue my role if I moved to Arizona, but I'd rather stick my head in an oven than live there. I decided to take my severance package and seek other jobs. I decided that I didn't want to do the corporate America thing and started my own business and sold window treatments, which was a trade I had learned from my father. That gig was boring me. It's like my father always said, "When you have your own business, you have no one to blame and no one to thank." So, I took a part-time job at a shop that sold fabrication and installation services for natural stone. It was a mom and pop kind of business. I started to become really miserable and frustrated with my lack of career progress. I desperately wanted was a professional sales role and opportunity with an organized company.

I would continue to research open sales positions in the very limited job market in my area. Going on job interviews on a weekly basis was really exhausting. I was becoming real bitter and cynical. I hated the injustice of the fact that I would get an invitation to interview for lame jobs that was commission only with a lame product or service that just wanted to create on army of aimless sales reps. I couldn't afford to take a commission only job at that point, either. I was becoming bitter at the fact that when there were jobs I was really interested in they did not offer the position to me or when they were about to they would change their minds at the last minute and offer the position to someone else. I was at the end of my rope.

I had seen a job posted on monster.com. The job description was just what I was looking for and it seemed like a perfect match except for one somewhat major detail. The sales job was for the senior care industry. Seniors? I didn't even know that there was a career created along those lines. Oh sure, there are lots of diverse or different sales jobs out there, but working with or for seniors? I figured what the hay? I submitted my resume and figured my career as an interviewee was my current role in life and you never know where an interview will take you.

One of the natural laws in life is when it rains, it pours. I had some interesting interviews that I was getting excited about. Then one evening in March 2004 I got a phone call at around seven o'clock and everything changed. Some Sales Manager named Mitch called to conduct a brief phone interview. My initial thoughts were that this was some lame company and probably a glorious multi-level-marketing opportunity. I was downright cynical and real bitchy on the phone. I figured that I didn't have time for this. I got right down to the most important question.

I asked about the monetary compensation. The base pay and commission sounded really reasonable. Mitch seemed like a decent guy and someone I would be interested in meeting. So, I met Mitch at the local office at the senior care company and enjoyed our time together. Mitch is a straight shooter. He didn't pause at all when I asked a question which told me he was the kind of guy that didn't have anything to hide. Mitch was more interested in thoroughly explaining the position, industry, company and selling the position to me which was a refreshing twist to the grueling interview process.

After our interview, Mitch wanted to know what I thought about the position. It sounded intriguing to me. My interest was piqued. The next step was for me to meet with the Executive director and if all went well I would then spend a day in the field with a current representative in the local office. I indicated that I was interested to move forward with the next step and we scheduled an interview with the Executive Director, Janey.

CHAPTER 3 – I'M NOT SURE I'M CUTOUT FOR THIS

I interviewed with Janey. Her long lineage of Scottish ancestors blessed her with long slender legs, ice chip blue eyes and white hair. This woman was born with a classy look. One that I would take full advantage of down the road. I found her to be intimidating. I later discovered that she was slightly shy at times. My perception of her was wrong. Janey was a little balls to the wall with me. Maybe she herself was getting exhausted from conducting interviews. She was adamant about one thing. Janey didn't want to hire anyone that wouldn't commit to staying in the position for at least two years.

My longest duration of employment to that point was my three and half years at the telecom company. My personal relationships were with my ex-boyfriend that I had moved to California with. We lasted a total of six years. I had recently ended a three year relationship with my second long term boyfriend. I can be very loyal once I commit to something, but her words gave me a pain in my gut. I'm an Aries. Like I said, once I commit to something I am super loyal. It's just getting there that is the hard part. I am a little commitment phobic and I never like being told what to do.

I agreed to the commitment if hired and set up a day to go in the field with the current sales rep. My day was to be spent with the rep that had been there for about two years. She was at least fifteen years older than me. I instantly connected to her. She had grown up in New York and had an east coast vibe that I really enjoyed. I liked her sense of humor and she was eager to explain the business to me.

I can't remember all the visits that day, but one memory was specifically vivid. We went to visit a tri-level senior community. For those of you that are getting an education for the first time a tri-level community is one that includes three components; Independent, Assisted Living, and a Skilled Nursing Facility (SNF). Independent and Assisted sections can vary depending on the senior community, but the SNFs are typically the same.

An independent community will usually offer a choice of a home that could be an independent structure or something similar to an apartment or condo. There will probably be a clubhouse or recreation area in which a variety of activities could be planned for residents. Monthly fees could potentially pay for services such as housekeeping and maintenance, but meals are usually not included. There may or may not be a "buy in" to the community. A "buy in" could be waived or cost as much as over one hundred thousand dollars depending on the type and location of the community.

An Assisted living community will consist of multi-unit componenents that could provide assistance with medications and daily activities such as bathing, dressing, laundry, and general housekeeping. There could be transportation services or activities as well. The level of services and costs associated with any of services or supplemental services is dependent on that community.

The SNF or rehabilitation facility is what it is. They are facilities licensed to provide skilled nursing services under the supervision of licensed nurses. They will have rehabilitative services for people who will eventually gain their physical independence and could potentially return to their homes or they will never return and their long term plan will remain in a skilled nursing residence until they pass away.

The advantage to moving into a senior community with the tri-levels is so that you can AGE IN PLACE. You will have limited need to leave the community should your physical and cognitive limitations progress. The advantage to aging in place and being in a tri-level community is also so that you have a guaranteed "bed" or space in the SNF if you should need it one day. If you have any idea at all about the options of SNFs you would know that it is an option and choice that you do want control over. This will become more apparent as I navigate you through the senior care industry.

Upon our visit to the community I was getting a general education about the industry. The company I was interviewing for was involved in senior care, but not necessarily in a senior community. This company provided supportive services and solutions to enable people to remain in their own homes or their current independent settings. The company provided custodial services on a physical and emotional level with a high level of professional oversight. The professional oversight was what really separated this company apart from others.

We proceeded to meet a contact at the community to provide a tour. This tour was conducted to gain a general overview of this particular community. Of course, we were visiting the community so I could get more educated on the industry, but there are many other reasons as well. This is your first introduction to my personal experiences as well as your introduction to the business side of the industry. This is your introduction to how it all works.

You see the bigger picture of this, is that this senior community is looking for referrals. They are seeking residents and our company could very well be a referral source for them. This community or the contact conducting the tour could likely be a resource for a senior care or home care company. They can refer people not necessarily ready to take the plunge and live in a senior community. They could also refer our company to residents that require outside or supplemental home care in any of their tri-level components.

There is another very important component to this industry. It is regarding the people who suffer from dementia. Dementia or Alzheimer's disease. They are not the same. Just because someone has a diagnosis of dementia, it doesn't necessarily mean they have Alzheimer's disease. Dementia is a cognitive disorder. Dementia is a non-specific illness and affects areas of cognition which could affect memory, attention, language and problem solving. There are hundreds of forms of dementia. And in case you didn't know, at this given time the only way to determine if anyone really has Alzheimer's disease is if you do an autopsy on their brain.

During my tour of the senior community we proceeded to the Alzheimer's/Memory care unit. We walked along the hall and I saw a variety of residents. Some were engaged in a group activity with a facilitator. I noticed a large glass case filled with happy birds. I think -that's nice. I love birds. How cute! Our tour guide points out a woman in a side room. She was standing over an ironing board. She is old, fragile, delicate and soft moving in her actions.

The tour guide says, "The resident in that room is Emily. Emily is almost one hundred years old. She insists on doing her own ironing. The care giver in there is assisting her." Well, that is bittersweet, I thought to myself.

Then my head turned to a room where a man is propped up in a bed. His mouth open and he was still and looking into space. Do you have any idea what a man that is immobile, unaware of his surroundings, barely existing and having limited mobility, communicative or cognitive skills looks like? Have you ever seen anyone sitting patiently waiting for death to come wrap their arms around them and take them to a place of peace? A wave of emotion moved through me and I felt my eyes fill up with tears.

Our tour guide noticed my discomfort and very empathetically said, "It can be a difficult thing to witness if you don't have experience with this type of existence".

My last interview with the company included Mitch, Janey, and Anna who was the V.P. of Operations. They asked me a series of questions. None of which I remember except for the last few questions.

Anna asked, "Jessica, what do you think would be the challenges in this position for you?"

I replied, "You indicated that I would have to coordinate and conduct group presentations that could involve PowerPoint applications. I have no experience in that area, but I am willing to learn."

Anna asked, "Is that all? Is there anything else?"

I said, "Well, there is a huge emotional component to this position. I think that would be challenging to overcome".

Anna said, "Is that all? Do you have any additional questions?"

I then said, "Yes. I do have another question. Did anyone ever tell you that you look like Kate Hudson?" I really thought that Anna had an uncanny resemblance to the actress Kate Hudson. I then looked at Janey and said, "And you look like Pricilla Presley". I really thought she did.

Mitch said, "Who do I look like? Chris Farley?" Mitch doesn't really look like Chris Farley. Although, he does look like a football coach and he was just the coach I was looking for. Mitch was a real sales coach.

A few days later I received emails from Anna and Mitch. They both thanked me for my time and indicated there interest in me and the hopes that I would make the decision to join their team. I figured that they saw something in me and they were convinced I was a good match and would be a valuable addition to their company. Mitch called me about a week later. He was waiting for my final decision. I drilled Mitch with a ton of questions. He answered all of them and then I said, "Sign me up, Buttercup". My whole life changed forever and for the better.

CHAPTER 4 – YOUNG BLOOD

I was eager to start my new job although I delayed it until one day after my 30th birthday. I did a Vegas trip with some girlfriends and my sister Julie and reported to my first day of work on a Tuesday. I met my new office colleagues and got my phone, office and schedule for the next few weeks. I still had my post weight loss as a result of my break-up from my second long term relationship so I was excited to parade my new skinny clothes as well.

In the first few weeks I visited our corporate office in Los Angeles. I visited some new colleagues and received training on the computer system, policies and company guidelines. The company was relatively smaller at the time so I even got the opportunity to have one-on-one training with the Chief Professional Officer, Tim, who was also the co-founder of the company. The other co-founder, Robert, was the Chief Executive Officer. There again I was in an organization with a real yin yang component.

The CEO is a decent guy. Robert is somewhat of typical CEO type. Robert kind of has a big ego, but you need that in a strong leader. He is originally from Boston. Did you know that over 50% of CEOs in the west coast are originally from the east coast? That makes perfect sense to me. I can't imagine anything getting done on the west coast otherwise, but that's just me. Now Tim is truly one of a kind. He is one of the smartest, quickest, articulate and sensitive men one will ever meet. He is downright brilliant sometimes. He is a true leader and advocate in the Geriatric Care Management community. He is an avid speaker and as this industry grows I believe he will be one of the most well-known and respected leaders in his field even more than he already is. I have the utmost respect and admiration for Tim.

I received about 2 days of one-on-one sales training with Mitch in my local office. I was excited to know that the training I was receiving had a monetary value of five thousand dollars. That's Mitch. ALWAYS creating value. I found him to be a great teacher and mentor. I was also shocked at how I was retaining the information and was alert through the duration of my training sessions. I have a real gift for day dreaming. If I could get paid for that I would be a billionaire. Although, it's kind of difficult to day dream when you are the only pupil.

I was ready to be unleashed. I am a natural hunter and researcher. More importantly, my greatest value in any area of my life is that I love to connect people and be a resource. I was going to shine in my new role. My main objective in the company is to find business and gain clients for the company. We are a referral based business. We could do a lot of advertising and marketing via the net and newspapers, but at the end of the day it comes down to getting direct referrals from a variety of professional sources.

Let's get down to what the business is all about and my role in the company. My title was Elder Care Consultant. I explain who my company is and what we do. We are a professionally led senior care company. Oh, there are tons of senior care companies and they come in lots of different forms. What separated our company from the rest was our model which is, was, and will always be the best model for a non-medical senior care company. Bar none. Our primary purpose is to facilitate a systematic approach to create solutions and options to help an elderly person(s) to remain in their own homes as independently as possible for as long as possible. That makes good sense, right?

Most people would like the option to stay in their own homes.

We not only provided care giving and custodial services from thoroughly screened and experienced care givers, but our model included a Geriatric Care Manager to assess, create, and oversee a care plan. The Care manager supervises and orients the care givers, advocates for the client, is a liaison for all professionals, family and contacts involved. The Care Manager assists in creating a safe, efficient, and creative care plan and their on-going oversight ensures continuity of care. Sounds good, right? Well, the model is very efficient. Does the model always work? Sure, except when you put people in the mix. It's not a perfect world and many times we're dealing with a whole lot of people that are very far from perfect so this industry certainly has its challenges.

My company unleashed me and I was ready to explore in my new role and sell this fabulous service and just knock the socks off everyone's feet. One of my first tasks was to shop other companies and to make a few phone calls and inquire about services. I encourage anyone to do this if you are slightly curious. I was downright appalled at some of the companies. Some numbers went into a voicemail. Some never called back. When some called back I could barely hear them or even understand their broken English. I got burned out after the seventh call and then I was even more super excited about my new position. I felt like this would be a piece of cake. The competition out there was really no competition at all. I really thought this due to my experience with shopping around and our company model, so that's why when people asked me who our competitors are I confidently always replied with, "We have no competition."

I went to a few networking meetings and met some of the

industry peeps. One or two people were genuinely nice and the others were not so much. The industry starts to form their own cliques. The other challenge is that I was in an industry with the majority of my contacts were women. You know how caddy and competitive women can be. It is probably over seventy five percent women. That's before I started migrating into other referral sources such as lawyers and financial professionals. So, the other thing about these women is that they were veterans in this industry. They knew their stuff and I don't think little, petite, attractive, thirty year old Jessica was very appealing to them. I think they were less than impressed and they were not overall very friendly.

I learned just how unimpressed people were of me when I put on my high heel shoes and marched into their place of business all full of piss and vinegar with my company's service and ready to blow their minds with some new found information or concept. I was put in my place relatively quickly and although it was done in somewhat of a cruel manner it was a much needed lesson to learn.

On two occasions when I visited a SNF and I was giving my over enthusiastic sales pitch I was completely not in tune with my audience. I was so focused on my sales role and sales objectives that I didn't acknowledge what the big picture was and that I was lacking in areas of industry knowledge and the fundamental basics of building relationships. I was given the lesson quickly which put a halt to my one woman show and my one way perspective.

After I gave my pitch, my diplomatic and less than impressed contact asked me if I would like a tour of the facility. I was starting to wonder why they gave Skilled Nursing Facilities the acronym SNF. That's the last thing you want to do is take a sniff.

If you could hold your breath through the duration of the visit it would be a less much miserable experience. Also, the fact that the facilities are also called Convale*scent* hospitals was a mystery to me as well. It's not just the scent of bodily fluids such as urination and defecation that hit you like a ton of bricks, but depression, anxiety, fear and lingering death all have their own scents as well.

The end of my tour would bring me to a room where someone was in a hospital bed and barely hanging on to life. Barely hanging on by a bitter thread or a life line as strong as a strand of hair. My tour guide would discreetly look at me and I would have this very non-chalant response with my words and body language. I was keeping my thoughts and emotions at bay. It's something I was convincing myself I had to do in order to overcome a challenging emotional component to my new career. I had closed my heart and my empathetic mind and these tour guides were in their own way giving me a chance to see the light and the importance to staying human and to embrace all humans I encountered. We all need and deserve a human touch.

I may be inexperienced and uneducated in some areas, but I am not stupid and I am highly intuitive. I was rather uneasy about my visits and I wanted to make sure I was doing a good job and the last thing I wanted to do was leave a negative impression of myself and the company I worked for and now represented. I told Janey about my experience. I gave her a step by step play of my encounters.

I asked Janey if she thought that I was brought to those patients' rooms on purpose and she simply replied with, "Yes. It sounds like they were doing that on purpose".

Well, lesson learned and I was never going down that

corridor again.

CHAPTER 5 – HELLO, NORMA JEAN

I went out into the field and started to make contact with some of the agencies and supportive services that catered or was somehow connected to seniors. I went to visit a staff member of the Hospice organization. At the ripe age of thirty I probably should have had some clue or idea of hospice, but I really had none. I find that I was somewhat fortunate in the fact that I had no experience with someone very close to me that had died. My grandparents on my father's side had already passed away before I was born, and my grandfather was in Florida at the time when he passed and I was 15 at the time. My parents did not share all the details surrounding the progression of Pa's death. My grandmother had passed away after I had moved to California.

I met with a very sweet hospice counselor named Joanie. Joanie uncovered the services of hospice. There are typically two components of hospice. One component assists with the medical and custodial services which create care plans for the actively dying on a physical level. The other supportive services are to assist people on the psycho social and emotional level. Joanie worked for the later component of hospice and conducted individual and group counseling for the actively dying and the surviving parties of those individuals both pre and post death. There are also counseling services for those who are survivors of victims of homicide or relatives and personal contacts of people that committed suicide.

I was pretty blown away. Joanie explained the services with such ease and handled me, as I am sure with all others, with extreme and gentle care. Joanie explained how death was part of the cycle of life. She has such a comforting way about her and it really helped me understand how amazing hospice is and the staff members that are a part of it. Joanie also was able to put my mind at ease and release some of my own personal fears about death. Upon departing from my visit with Joanie she embraced me and gave me a warm, sincere hug. God bless Joanie and everyone at hospice.

One of my next tasks was to spend time in the field with a Care Manager and do a home visit to one of our clients. I traveled with our Care Manager Patty to a town about 35 minutes north of our office. Patty and I got to know one another. She shared her information about her education which was mainly medical. Patty has a nursing background and in addition to care managing she is also a Parish nurse. Patty also has an interesting hair style. The best way to describe it is to say that it is really big and I think she single handedly keeps the aerosol companies in business. Patty comes from a big family which I think contributes to her amazing talent of mass producing food dishes that could feed an army. She was really appreciated when we had potluck parties in the office.

Upon arriving at the client's home Patty had explained that the client was unhappy about the fact that there was a care giver in her home. The client did not want the care giver there. Patty's role is to manage these types of issues and secure continuity of our services. Patty also indicated that the client had a good rapport with her and that she trusted her so she felt relatively confident that she would be able to stabilize the situation. Patty bought me some lunch so that we could get better acquainted and then we proceeded to the client's home.

Patty knocked on the door. The door opened and there she was, Norma. I was taken back when I saw her. Norma looked just like my grandmother, Ma. I mean the resemblance was uncanny. Norma was wearing dark royal blue pants and a white short sleeved button down collared shirt that had light blue stripes with little blue flowers with green stems and leaves throughout. Norma resembled Ma, but she looked like she generally lived a healthier and happier life. You can tell by a person's smile lines. She had Ma's hair, too. It was whiter and generally the same style when Ma's hair looked nice.

Patty and I entered Norma's home. You knew she was not very happy, but I think it was tough for her to maintain her unhappy composure when she saw Patty. Patty and Norma exchanged some words and I think Norma explained her discomfort with the fact that there was a stranger in her home and she didn't want her to be there. Patty indicated that she and the care giver were going to talk in the other room and I stayed in the kitchen with Norma. We sat at her kitchen table together and we had a little chat. I couldn't believe that in addition to the uncanny resemblance to Ma, Norma herself was originally from New York. So, on top of everything else, she sounded just like Ma.

Norma asked, "What is your name?"

I replied, "Jessica."

Norma said, "I don't know why this stranger has to be in my home. I don't want this stranger in my home. Look at my home. I keep it very clean. I take care of everything myself. I can take care of myself. I can clean my own home. Do you see how clean my home is?"

I said, "Your home is very clean. It is a lovely home."

Norma asked, "Do you know why they are here in my home? I just want to be alone. I want to take care of myself. I don't want a stranger in my home with me."

I replied, "I am not certain, but I am sure Patty will alleviate your concerns. She will be back in a few minutes."

Norma and I continued to chat. She seemed perfectly fine to me. Norma was very neat and clean in appearance and her home was immaculate. Norma seemed perfectly capable to me. She appeared physically fit. Norma really didn't let up about her discomfort about the current living arrangements during the duration of the conversation. Then I started thinking to myself – this woman does not appear to need help with bathing, dressing, cooking or cleaning. I wasn't completely confident to be driving on the same road as her, but her fabulous Mercedes in the garage was in very good condition so I figured when she was in a better state of mind Norma could pull it together if she had to. What in god's name is going on here? What kind of company was I working for? Who the hell do I report my company to? Do I call the police? I recently learned about Adult Protective Services (APS). Do I call them?

Then Norma asked me, "What's your name?"

I replied, "Jessica."

Norma and I continued to chat. We talked about whatever. We talked about her car, her immaculate home, her discomfort about the care giver.

Then Norma asked, "What's your name?"

I replied, "Jessica."

Okay, so the first couple of times it didn't seem too weird to me. Norma was under a lot of stress and maybe she wanted to make sure she had my name correct. After about the fifteenth time that Norma asked what my name was I started to get the bigger picture here. Norma's need for support was not necessarily on a physical level. Although Norma looked like she was as fit as a woman could be at her age, her issues were apparently deeper.

Patty returned to the kitchen table and started talking to Norma and politely attempted to help her understand her current living situation. Now, over the years I have learned plenty more and even today I am not sure that I agree with Patty's method, but I am in no position to judge her method of care management. I still to this day would be at a loss on how to re-direct someone like Norma in a similar situation.

Patty said, "Norma, you have a problem with your brain. You have a disorder."

Norma was taken off guard. She said surprisingly, "I do? What am I going to do? Can we go to the doctor?"

Patty said, "We already went to the doctor."

Norma said, "Can we get medicine? Can we get medicine for my problem?"

Patty said, "We already have medicine for you."

At that moment Norma's face completely changed. She seemed defeated. A defeated expression slowly covered her face and then her eye lids become heavy. Norma's defensive posture became softened and she began to slouch. At that moment, Norma's meds kicked in.

The purpose of Patty's visit was successful. Patty was able to stabilize the situation and create a more manageable environment that would be synergetic at least for a little while. The care giver seemed appreciative and relieved. I said good bye to Norma. Patty gave the care giver some additional instructions and then we left Norma's home. As Patty and I started to walk back to Patty's car I found it difficult to hide my emotions. I was on the verge of tears when we sat back in Patty's car.

Patty said, "When we get back to the office you can go home."

I was even more saddened to learn about Norma's history. She was a widow. Her very handsome son, who by the glamour shot and photos in the home seemed to be linked to the entertainment industry, had died a few years ago. Norma's closest surviving relative was her brother that still resided in Long Island and he himself was suffering from dementia. Norma was conserved, meaning the legal system had a court appointed conservator to manage Norma's finances and health related decisions. Norma did not have the mental capacity to care for herself.

In addition, Norma's neighbors had been financially abusing her. They convinced her to sign her home, automobile, and finances over to them. Norma is one of thousands of victims of financial abuse. Thankfully, our legal system intervened and was able to provide protection and security for Norma. Her maniac low life neighbors consistently tried to call, visit, and manipulate Norma. Finally, with much help from my company and Norma's conservator she was transitioned to a memory care unit at a senior living community. I continued to visit Norma in her new home for the following five years.

6 – SALES 101

I was a few weeks into my job and I was really enjoying it. Well, not every single part of it. For instance, I had to attend weekly meetings with the staff where they reviewed each individual case and client. It was time well served to get a deeper understanding of how the model works and the roles of the staff members that also included our recruiting and staffing department. It was about all I could handle when someone started talking about bodily fluids and really unfortunate health conditions.

I asked Mitch, "I just want to know how necessary it is to participate in all the staff meetings? I really don't think it is necessary. I think I get the gist of it."

Mitch said, "Well, most of the sales people attend the meetings. Why don't you want to attend?"

I replied, "Well I just don't really think I need to hear about suppositories, diarrhea or how a penis was getting crusty around a catheter."

Mitch said, "Ok, I'll talk to Janey."

I learned very early how to get to the point with Mitch, you just get to the point. No point in tip toeing around it. At the end of the day, if you got something to say, just say it to Mitch. The man has the patience of a kid on Christmas morning waiting for their parents to wake up so they can open their gifts. In other words, he has very little patience. He has shut down my complaining and whining many a time by just asking, "Jessica, what do you want?"

I was getting a little more education than I cared to learn. I was in a tough spot. I was eager to sell, sell, sell. However, what did I really know? Not a whole lot and there is so much to know and learn. You learn every day and when you are open to it things come easier. I tried to protect myself and guarded the information from coming in too fast. There were some things I just wasn't ready to learn. I really just wanted to stay focused on the marketing component.

I wanted to focus on the fundamentals of selling and becoming an expert at it. I knew that I could sell, I just needed to hone in on my selling skills. I have had three really great sales mentors. Of course there is Mitch, who I will be forever grateful for the opportunity to work with and learn from him. There is my girlfriend Mona that I met later down the road and then there is my favorite teacher and mentor of all, my father, Marc Solomon.

When I was a kid my father was in the textile business and owned a retail store. I would often accompany my father when he went to work on Saturdays and we would also go "pick up goods" in New York city and New Jersey. I loved being my dad's co-pilot. I spent many a rides and days "at the store" with him. I assumed that my father was grooming me for the family business. I assumed it was a natural progression of things and then one day my father completely broke my heart. I think I was about nine years old and I had made a casual comment about when I would run the store in the future.

My father said, "You are not going to run the store when you grow up."

What? I thought - did my dad just say what I think he said? My next thought was -Well, who the hell is going to run the store?

My father could not possibly be considering running the business with one of my two older sisters and then gradually transition the business to them. I was the "smart one." I knew this for a fact because that was my label growing up. Don't you just love labels? But seriously, why the hell was I investing all this time in being a little apprentice?

I was a little shocked to say the least with this new information and said, "Well, who is going to run the store?"

I was getting ready to go into full on crazy mode if he picked my sister, Julie. I love Julie to death right now, but when I was younger I more wanted to fight her to death. We even had scheduled fight times. We got so used to fighting it rolled into organized fighting.

My father said, "I don't want you to run a store. I want you to go to college and have a career."

I couldn't think of anything else in the world that I wanted to do besides run my dad's business with him. I felt rejected by my father. Maybe he didn't think I could do a good job? Then I realized that could not possibly be it. After all, I was the "smart one". Where other kids may have suffered from low self-esteem, I suffered from high self-esteem. I got back on track and realized what I knew to be true and that is that my father is the smartest man in the world and he totally figured this out for me. I just wished he told me a little sooner so I would have realigned my future plans earlier.

So, my original future plans of Solomon & Daughter were out the window, but like a good young Jedi I stayed close to my father and learned everything that I could. I had to make a few modifications due to my obvious behavior traits, but I learned the most important basics in business. I accompanied him when he met with his business peeps and when he was out making deals and I listened to everything he said.

One lesson was to "keep your mouth shut." That may have been said to me more than a few times because I have a big mouth and keeping it shut was pretty much impossible so I had to make quite a few modifications on that one.

Next, "never steal from the hand that feeds you". Now, I may have on occasion taken some cookies home with me that went unsold when I was selling cookies at the mall kiosk, but not stealing from the hand that feeds you makes perfect sense. I never want my employer to take advantage of me, so why would I ever take advantage of them? You lie and cheat others and you are only lying and cheating yourself. I couldn't live with the guilt anyway.

"Don't go apeshit". In other words, don't get over excited about things. Don't lose your cool. I think that will always be a work in progress. I have definitely mellowed out over the years and become less emotional regarding work. Sometimes, on occasion, I may go a little apeshit, but I can mask that with an overly enthusiastic attitude.

"Not everything is black and white. Sometimes there is a shade of gray". Do I need to elaborate?

"NEVER burn your bridges. Never. You never tell anyone to F@$# off unless you know that you absolutely never want to see them ever again. You never know if you'll need to use them later in life" which brings us to "Don't get mad. Get even". Now, I am not always sure where my father is going with that one, because I've seen my Dad get angry, but Marc Solomon is no vigilante. My interpretation of that one for me is to not give someone your power. If someone does you wrong just walk away. Take the high road. Your character does not have to be depleted and will end up stronger and that is getting even. It's all about the balance of power.

"It's not what you say, it's what you do".

My all-time favorite and the absolute, undeniable, ultimate law and simple truth is, "It's not what you know, it's who you know." I am a natural connector. I love sales. I love to be a resource to people. My favorite thing to do is to connect to people and connect people with each other.

With all the basics down pat and now with Mitch under my wings I was gonna fly high. Mitch has a very unique managing style. It's not your typical sales management style at all. He is totally positive. Seriously, the man has selective hearing. Mitch cannot hear negativity, he goes deaf. Mitch focuses on your own style, the fabulous you that you are, and your positive attributes. Should you dare to be negative or go into a self-loathing tailspin, Mitch will blow so much sunshine up your butt that it will be downright painful to ever go down that road again. It's just not worth it. I listened to everything Mitch told me. Mitch's goal is to make his sales force better every day.

CHAPTER 7 – HONEY BUNNY

I was just a few days shy of one month into the new job. I was calling around town to set appointments to meet new contacts and potential referral sources. I look back now and I think how amazing I was at taking this job in full charge ahead mode, considering how little I knew at the time. But my middle name is persistence and at the end of the day, if truth be told, I am a cold calling whore. There are lots of successful sales people out there and they will tell you with all honesty that they never cold called a day in their life. For me, it's how I get re-charged. It's the thrill of the kill for me.

The bigger the challenge, the better. Put a big neon light that says NO SOLICITING in front of a door with flashing lights attached with a security system against sales people and I laugh. Chuckle to myself more like it. Regardless of the devices and protocol to prevent the likes of me getting through is just the challenge I am looking for. I shall not fear and I really don't. I am more concerned at what will happen after my successful sales call against all odds that it could actually be a success. I sometimes even get a little depressed after the success of my cold call. If I am successful then I have to start hunting for my next challenge.

My initial calls and appointments were at Assisting Living Communities and SNFs. It's easy to set appointments at Assisted Livings because they are eager to give you a tour of their community. After all, I and my fellow co-workers are a potential referral source for them. Now SNFs are a little more challenging. You could possibly call the Admissions coordinator for the same reason, they want referrals as well, but they generally get their business from a direct pipeline from the hospitals. What you are really looking to get in front of is the Discharge Planners in a hospital and a SNF.

Discharge planners are really tough to get in front of. They are super busy and they really don't have time for sales pitches. They have a ton of different vendors that are looking to get business from them. Some examples are durable medical equipment companies, medical home health, and residential care facilities for the elderly (RCFE) that are looking for referrals. Discharge planners probably care the least to hear or talk to someone like me trying to pitch them non-medical home health. We're private pay and we are generally not an accredited business. Discharge planners don't always feel that comfortable referring patients to something that is not covered by insurance, fairly expensive and is not monitored by a regulatory agency. I really can't blame them either.

I am at my desk in the office calling around and I called a SNF fairly close to the main hospital in town. I finally get a hold of the discharge planner and he is super reluctant to set up a meeting. Big surprise. Blah, blah, blah and his supervisor is out of town and he is even more busy than usual, but he sets a time to meet for 9:00 am that Friday.

So, this is around the same time I am still recovering from my last long term relationship and I was still knee deep in my post break-up/self-destructive party stage. I am amazed at all the energy I had to give to my new job and still would go out just about every night. My girlfriend convinced me that because we were single we were socially obligated to society to be out in the public eye in our free time. I was just about to order a margarita in honor of Cinco de Mayo in a very crowded and noisy bar and in walked my golden ticket.

Now some people are lucky, right? That could mean some people are unlucky. I don't really consider myself either. I believe there are no coincidences in life. I am not totally convinced that you create your own luck. Some sales people are better than others and there is no denying that. Although I believe that there are no coincidences and that perhaps it's just being at the right place at the right time. One might cough that up to luck. If that be the case, I just got pretty lucky.

This familiar face walks up to me and my girlfriend. I knew this guy from four degrees of separation. He was friends with the brother of my recently ex-boyfriend's best friend. We made some small talk. He started to loosen his tie and his composure and tried to relax from what looked like a tough day from work.

I said, "What are you doing these days?"

Mr. Golden Ticket takes a lavender business card out and hands it to me. The name of the business didn't sink in, but his job title did. The Job title was Discharge Planner. Well, it was at that moment that I knew who would be buying the rest of the cocktails. My order for a margarita drink was now going to be a pitcher and I proceeded to tell him what my new job was.

I then said, "Wait a minute. Didn't I just speak to you the other day?"

Golden Boy said, "Oh my god. You're the Jessica that's coming in tomorrow at 9am".

A few pitchers led to a few more hours of partying at Golden boy's house with my girlfriend and his roommate. Which led me to a slight hangover the next day, but I pulled it together for the 9am connection. I got a tour of the SNF and we really got down to business. Golden Boy was sharp and he is the kind of guy that would put one hundred percent into whatever job he had. He's got great work ethic, of course he does. He's originally from the east coast. We spoke the same language. Furthermore, he was intrigued with my position and ultimately saw himself in a sales position. Bottom line, he understands business and sales. Not your average discharge planner.

I continually visited the SNF and my golden ticket which I renamed Honey Bunny. I rarely called him by his real name and as many times as my father asked me when we were talking shop I still would not reveal his real name to my Dad. My father would always attempt to get it out of me.

The conversation will go something like this.

Dad: You know that convalescent hospital you visit?

Me: Yeah

Dad: You know that one that your friend works at?

Me: Uh Huh

Dad: You know that guy?

Me: Who?

Dad: That guy?

Me: You mean Honey Bunny?

Dad: Yeah, him. What's his name?

Me: Honey Bunny

Dad: I know, but what's his name?

Me: Honey Bunny.

Seriously, it's been years, but you can repeat the same conversation verbatim. My dad never gives up. Awesome. Maybe that's where some of my persistence comes from?

Another important turn for the better was meeting Honey Bunny's boss, Jo-Ann. Honey Bunny said we would totally hit it off. And boy, did we ever. Jo-Ann is truly one of a kind. She is a very sassy Italian from New Jersey. Jo-Ann is around fifty and I would confidently bet money that there are few twenty year olds that have half the energy Jo-Ann has even on one of her low energy days. Jo is super passionate about physical therapy and can fine tune just about anyone on both a physical and emotional level. Emotions and state of mind is just half the battle in physical therapy.

Now just so you know, it's not common for people from Jersey and people from New York to fall in love with each other. Some people in the north east would consider the Tapanzee or George Washington bridges equivalent to the Gaza strip in the Middle East. Back there is an unspoken rivalry between New Yorkers and Jersey folks and just so you know, New Yorkers win every time. It's the law. I am convinced that the first three words anyone from New Jersey learns is; Mama, Dada, and douchebag. However, in the west coast there is an instant connection between East Coasters, particularly if you are originally from the New England area. I can't explain it, but it's like smelling your mother's cooking on a holiday. It just feels like home.

Part of my weekly routine was just hanging around the SNF. I would do pop-ins. I would do coffee runs. I would get a call from Honey Bunny or Jo and they would say, "It's feeling like an iced blended mocha day". I would be there within fifteen minutes with four double cupped ice blended mochas with straws and muffins for everybody. It was no problem. I was happy to do it.

I walked in wearing a coat that Jo liked and she said, "Ooooo, I love that coat. "Would love that in pink".

No problem! I ran down to the department store, bought it, and then brought it to her work so she could try it on. If Jo liked it she would of course reimburse me. The coat didn't fit her so I returned it. The point was that I was creating value. Probably not exactly what Mitch had in mind when he taught that lesson, but nonetheless I was creating value. It just had a Jessica spin to it.

I was Honey Bunny's transportation after work when he became Honey Bunny sans car. When Honey Bunny's girlfriend came to town I used my local connections to help get him a deal for a hotel or dinner. I became a real Johnny-on-the spot and I was damn good at it, if I do say so myself. I was having a blast, too. I was really enjoying my job and I was starting to make really great new friends. In the east coast they say, "When you make a friend, you make a friend for life." Jo-Ann is a friend for life.

CHAPTER 8 – GETTING A REAL EDUCATION

Despite my efforts of being the coolest sales rep ever we can't deny the fact that although home care is a very serious and a much needed component to the healthcare industry, it wasn't the coolest and sexist sales job out there. I was going to have to become more educated about the industry and I was going to have to learn about the hard facts and sad realities of the people we cared for and their debilitating circumstances.

I attended conferences organized by the Alzheimer's Association. It's there I began to learn about the different forms of dementia and the nature of Alzheimer's disease. I learned about Sundowner's syndrome which is a condition often associated with the early stages of Alzheimer's. People that suffer from the syndrome could experience periods of extreme agitation and confusion during the late afternoon or early evening hours. I have seen this behavior with residents at Assisted Living communities in dementia units.

All I could really think about now was how I am going to be a Sundowner. I just know it. If I should ever suffer from dementia I think there is a high probability that I could end up with sundowner's syndrome. I base this on the fact that I have always been super sensitive to light. It's a strong reason why I choose to live in Central California. I am solar powered. Also, my mother says that when I was a baby I was perfectly wonderful until 4pm and I became an uncontrollable and inconsolable monster for an hour. It happened every evening. To this day when the sun starts setting I seem to get a second wind out of nowhere.

I attended an Elder Abuse conference and learned about

the seven types of elderly abuse. They are neglect, physical, sexual, financial, violation of basic rights, psychological, and self-neglect. Did you know the biggest form of elderly abuse is financial? Did you know that the majority of the abusers are family members? It's true. On some occasions it's not that intentional. You cannot imagine the false sense of entitlement some people have. It's downright sickening.

On another elder abuse conference I attended they focused a little more about sexual abuse. They explained that inmates in prisons discuss and compare notes on how easy it is to prey on the frail and elderly. They coined the phrase, "gerofiles". Oh, it gets worse. We listened to a case study about an eighteen year old male that raped a woman well into her eighties. If the visual in your mind isn't giving you a clear enough picture I'll have you know that on a projector screen which was about 6 feet by 6 feet they displayed a close-up shot of the eighty year old's abused and violated vagina.

Needless to say, I was rather shocked and somewhat nauseated. I appeared to be more shocked than anyone. I think this because I was looking all over the room to see some other person's shocked or horrified expression. I got nothing. I thought I was going to shoot up straight from my chair with my fists clenched and say, "What am I taking crazy pills? Is everybody seeing this?" I really got no validation on my thoughts from the audience. That was my last attendance at an elderly abuse conference. Besides the fact that I saw no real potential business from the attendees from my participation at the conference and also due to the fact that I can't sit still for more than twenty minutes and I'd rather stick a fork in my eye. I decided I would get my education from my work experience rather than a seminar.

Most of my continued education did come from my on the job experiences. Besides that, my company had all the information or connections to information that I would ever need regarding senior care. All other stuff I would have to wing it. My co-workers were super supportive of this. I would clearly misspell and mispronounce things. I never did have a keen sense of hearing. It took me a while just to get Coumadin down. I thought it was something like coometden. And after saying it about 300 times I still didn't know what is was and I didn't want to know. I was too afraid to ask. Just in case you are curious, it is a medication. It's a blood thinner.

I would continue to visit Jo-Ann and watch her do her magic on the rehab patients. You got to understand this generation of elderly we are caring for. They break a hip, they go to rehab, they get a tune-up, and then if all goes successful they return home. The thing that rehab tries to instill in them is how very important it is to continue the exercise regime that they are receiving in physical therapy. You know –keep the blood pumping. Keep the range of motion going. They usually give back a blank stare. The only exercise these folks were used to in their younger years was lifting their gin and tonic up and down from the table to their mouth. Oh, I forgot about the other arm. That one was used for their cigarettes.

One time I visited Jo and she was helping a man to rise from his wheelchair and take a few independent steps. Jo-Ann was helping him with stand-by assist and had her hand on his gait belt which was around his waist or chest or where ever you think it might be. So, I was standing about six feet in front of him with my everyday cuter can be and way too hot for senior care sales outfit.

Jo-Ann said, "See that pretty girl? I want you to try to walk up to her."

I stretched my arm in front of me and gave him a come hither wave with my hand and said, "Come to mama." I think I got a few more steps out of him.

One time the roles were slightly reversed. Jo-Ann was a few feet in front of a man that was rising from a wheel chair and walking towards her. I was in back of the wheelchair and Jo-Ann said, "Jess, Would you slowly move the chair behind him if he needs to sit down?"

I sure did. As the gentleman made progress I slowly moved the wheelchair behind him. I had to also slowly move the urine filled catheter bag that had slipped from the where it was supposed to be attached and it was dragging on the floor with his slow pace. I slowly pushed the bag with my black patent leather high heel shoes. I am not sure how embarrassed he was or if he was embarrassed at all. I mean, I was slightly embarrassed, but it's not a big deal. It is what it is. That's the reality. That's the humbleness of it all. Humble for the man that is receiving his treatment, humbleness for me that should just embrace this man for his courage, strength and ambition to get well and independent. I was honored to help.

Sometimes I would meet with potential clients and their family members. Meeting with adult children and family members was easy. Meeting with a married couple was a cinch, too. I loved to meet couples. I loved to hear about how they met. I heard the most romantic stories about couples that you would think came out of a romance novel or a movie. Couples who met in the service or met on trains. I got a play by play account of their first meeting and what happened for the next sixty years. I would be mesmerized and hypnotized with the stories. I would have to snap out of it when their attitude was like – can we get on with this already?

One time I found myself talking to a couple that wanted to just collect some information regarding home care services. The husband had a stroke and was sitting in wheel chair in the hospital room and his wife was sitting on the bed next to him. They were both feeling apprehensive about his return to home and were considering hiring some assistance at least for the first few days. They were a really sweet couple. During our conversation the gentleman sneezed and oh holy hell mother of god! It looked like half his brain shot out on his shirt. I did an immediate 180 degree turn to go get some tissues from the bathroom. I could barely manage to do this because in the process of trying to assist him I was dry heaving the whole time. I am truly sorry, but I just could not help it. It was an involuntary reaction.

Now meeting with individuals on a one on one basis is not my forte. I couldn't get it down. One of the Care managers I work with has a Social work background and would try to tell me that I was going too fast.

She would say, "You're going at like eighty five miles an hour and they are going at about fifteen miles an hour. Slow it the hell down."

I couldn't. I still don't think I can. I would very politely and sometimes not so politely get kicked out of a hospital room. I just couldn't connect. This could also be a reflection of my age. I just wasn't going to win over a crabby old woman, wasn't gonna happen. I would get excused from a room and then my Care

Manager would walk in and when she walked out twenty minutes later she relayed that she had the woman prepared to receive our services. Just like that. The care managers are really skilled at what they do.

Now, an older gentleman, that's where I stood a chance. Although, it's a wonder how I ever accepted a sales job in senior care because I have such a weakness for old men. My friend would tease me when we would go out for breakfast because I could not bear to see an older gentleman sitting at a counter by himself. It just tears me up inside. I am not sure why, it just does.

The same care manager also explained to me that dirty young men turn into dirty old men. It's so true. Sometimes our Care Managers or care givers would get groped. Some clients would grab a breast every chance they got. I was once touring a memory care unit and turned a corner to see a very happy man standing in the hallway. He was probably very happy that he was walking around with no pants on. For some odd reason, demented patients that had past occupations as firemen love to mark their territory, if you know what I mean. Go figure.

I was once walking up to a SNF and two men were sitting on a bench outside. I always smile especially to older gentleman and when I smiled to these men one of them said, "Hello."

I, of course, smiled and replied, "Hello" and kept walking.

I then overheard the one that did not say hello say to the other man, "You don't know her!"

Then they continued to argue about it. It wasn't exactly how I imagined two men fighting over me, but nonetheless I was flattered.

I was moving and grooving in my new position. Making the connections, closing some deals and getting some client cases. I was starting to earn more money and my client base and referrals were growing. Now Mitch might say that I am money motivated. That is true to some extent. I do sales. I get paid to make money. I get paid to make things happen. And it's true that we all do like to earn more money, of course. I had a commissioned component to my job and that's a part of sales. You generate more business and you earn more money. I do like money; however, I think I was more driven at being the best I could be. I thrive on success and to me, the monetary rewards are a reflection of my success and how well I do my job. I am driven by success and recognition.

Against my better judgment I continued to participate on weekly meetings with the staff in my office. I really didn't have that much choice in the matter in the beginning anyway. One day we were in the middle of a meeting and one of the Care Managers casually informed the staff that one of our clients died earlier that morning. Death is a part of this business. People die every day. I was getting used to that. What I wasn't getting used to was the sudden impact that a death had on my commission and sales quota.

I was annoyed to say the least and not very empathetically said, "What?!"

Janey looked at me and said, "I know what you are thinking and have a little sympathy."

I got Janey's message loud and clear. I was embarrassed at how I reacted. Janey taught me a lot without saying any words as well. The best way to describe Janey is that she is cool as a cucumber. She is in no way made of stone. She just doesn't sweat the small stuff. Janey has a real smooth approach to everything and she rarely overacts to anything or loses her cool. I've never seen her go apeshit. Janey is very even tempered.

Early in my career Janey accompanied me on some sales calls and meetings. I needed her support since she had oodles more experience in this field and having her present in these meetings not only served as an educational purpose for me, but it also added credibility to our company. Sometimes certain professionals with bigger egos liked the interaction with someone like Janey who was an Executive Director and at the upper management level. Janey also has a very classy look and is a classy lady. I often consult with my mother as a proper etiquette advisor and I consult with Janey when it comes to determining whether something may or may not be tacky.

During my time with Janey she shared some of her past work experiences. Like when she first started her nursing career and one of her first tasks was to just hold and nurture a baby that was abused. Do you have any idea how soft babies' bones are and that it takes a tremendous amount of force to break a baby's bone? Just about every bone was broken in that baby's body. I can't even imagine what that was like. I pray that baby grew up healthy and is loved and has a good life.

Janey talked about when she was a nurse in the hospital and was present at the time of a particular patient's death. Janey said the man was very sweet and loving and had a tremendous amount of love and support from his family during the time of his death. She said when the man crossed over that there was actually light that filled the room. It was a very bitter sweet experience to be present with that man and his family.

Janey also spoke about a woman who refused to die and tried to cheat death as best she could. The woman was hanging by a thread, had stopped eating and against all biological laws refused to die. Staff members in the hospital attempted to call her son and begged him to come to the hospital to forgive his mother and help her move on. The son would refuse and would hang up on the hospital staff. This woman must have been some type of evil. A Buddhist staff member came to her room to chant and then the woman would pant and groan. When Janey tries to reenact the woman's response you can't help to think she was possessed and the hairs on the back of my neck stand up.

Janey and I had toured a memory care unit together. There was a woman that was slouched over in her chair. Janey knelt down before her and started to caress her arm and her back. It was with such warmth and sincerity. Much like the time when Janey and I visited a woman in a hospital room and the woman was lying in bed and in need of oxygen and it was apparent to Janey that the tubes that were supposed to feed her oxygen had slipped down closer to her mouth and Janey very gently slipped the tubes back into the woman's nostrils.

After hearing Janey's stories, watching her, and visiting all these facilities and communities where people are providing physical support you can't help to wonder what you can do to make a difference and help in your own way. I knew I wasn't cut out to be a care giver and I wasn't signing up for nursing school any time soon, but I felt compelled to do something. In this industry there are endless amounts of opportunities to make a difference and serve people in need.

As I started to learn more about this industry I gained an education about a variety of non-profit organizations all of which are usually in dire needs of volunteers. I have prior experience in volunteering. Some of my experiences were at a food bank during the holidays to organize canned foods. I've watched children at the temple during Yom Kippur services. For a few years I would volunteer at the local zoo and I would annually join efforts to support zoo projects to make the grounds cleaner and more efficient. I went to the zoo solo on my 29th birthday and I am proud to point out the lattice concrete path that I helped construct with a team of people.

I dived into the non-profit world and made as much effort as I could to donate my time and I joined a number of committees. Some other seasoned professionals in my industry started to take a liking to me and gently forewarned me that if I wasn't careful I would be sucked into the non-profit vortex and I would be used as much as I allowed it and I should be aware of this and not to take on too much. I was embracing the fact that I felt so fortunate that I had a job that allowed me, on company time no less, to volunteer my time. It was such a feel good component to being a part of this industry.

Sooner or later I realized just how sucked in I got and I had to start making some boundaries. I was happy to help when and where I could, but I had to stay focused on what my job entailed and volunteering oodles of my time just was not going to make me or my company much money. Instead of volunteering all of my time I made an effort to find other volunteers. I often did this by encouraging the new people I started to meet in the industry that entered after me. Hey, that's how you learn.

Volunteering also had its danger risks. Like the time when I was a stage coordinator for a fundraising event for Alzheimer's disease. Hours before the event started I was getting ready in my very tiny bathroom and I dropped something in the narrow space between the sink and the wall. In my contorted position and in my effort to retrieve the dropped object I singed my left bicep with my curling iron. I don't know technically what kind of burn you would call it, but it was bad. It's almost five years later and you can still see the scar. I guess in my own way you can say that I fought in the battle against Alzheimer's. I have the battle wounds to prove it.

One day at work we had just received our weekly sales report from the corporate office and it was an extreme rare occasion where Janey lost her cool as cucumber composure. Janey was disturbed with the fact that our office had placed so low on the attrition rate compared to the other offices. I wasn't exactly sure why it was such a big deal considering our revenue was quite well at the time. I could have been missing something, because at the end of the day it's really about the revenue and although attrition had slipped due to an unfortunate amount of deaths and discharged patients we as an office were doing very well.

Janey was standing outside her office with the report in hand and stomped her foot, somewhat like a young girl that wasn't getting her way. I looked at Janey and saw this moment as an opportunity to share what she had taught me and give her back her own impactful words.

I said to Janey, "I know what you are thinking and have a little sympathy.

CHAPTER 10 – STAY FOCUSED

I was getting mucho enthusiastic about my job to say the least. I was still learning some things the hard way. One reason for learning the hard way is that I like to be independent and I have a real trial and error approach to things which led me to chasing imaginary rainbows with no pots of gold at the end and it was a real waste of time. I spent many a time in facilities that had oodles of not so potential clients. I spent lots of time marketing to facilities that weren't really ever going to produce clients that had the financial resources for our services.

I was trying to figure out where I was going wrong and maybe I should get a better idea of how Medicare and Medi-Cal worked. I kept hearing about it and I knew it had something to do with the reason some discharge planners would not refer, but I wasn't quite sure why. I was going to have to ask a lifeline. Back in the day I used to talk to Mitch quite a bit. I asked him about industry questions, sales techniques, and I have to admit I liked a little sunshine up my butt in the early days.

I said to Mitch, "I don't really understand the difference between Medicare and Medi-Cal".

Mitch replied, "uhhhhhh. Yeah. You want to try to avoid Medi-Cal."

I said, "Why? What does Medi-Cal mean?"

Mitch replied, 'Well, it basically means there's no money.'

Gotcha. Medi-Cal equals no money. Medi-Cal is California's Medicaid program. It provides health care coverage for low-income children and families as well as elderly, blind, or disabled individuals. Medi-Cal is jointly funded by the state and federal government, and administered by the California Department of Health Care Services. People enroll in Medi-Cal through their county social services department.

Are you to assume that everyone that is on Medi-Cal has little or no money? Well, sort of. For the most part. What if the person on Medi-Cal lives in a million dollar plus home, but all assets have been re-allocated so that the person can now apply for Medi-Cal? No one wants to drain their resources or lose an estate that may be promised to the relatives of that person, correct? Of course, not.

Look, I can't really judge and I can see in some instances where money may be tight or assets could be considerably drained depending on the long term care plan for an individual. Sometimes, someone will enter a SNF and "spend down" their assets because the SNF they are in will now be there home for the remainder of their life. They will have to apply for Medi-Cal and can't until they spend down all their assets.

But I really can't stand those sons of a bitchs that cheat the system and creatively re-allocate assets because they want to hold on to them when there are thousands of people in legitimate need. I can't stand the relatives with the unrealistic downright sickening false sense of entitlement. You know sometimes the more fortunate and wealthy are the worst. They think that they are so savvy and smart and the truth is that they are dumb shits and have no idea what they are doing and what limited options they just made their "loved ones". Take a little walk in a few Medi-Cal facilities. They are not serving champagne and caviar, ya know.

As much as people tried to return their loved ones back to their own homes from a SNF I would gently ask them to reconsider and asses if the person at the facility had long term medical or custodial needs. If there are limited financial resources or no resources left you better think twice. Think twice especially if they are in one of the better SNFs. Upon attempt for re-admittance there just might not be an available bed for that person the next time around. The availability just suddenly might not be there.

I have a buddy that is an Executive Director at an Assisted Living that is adjoined to a sister SNF. He was really perturbed by an arrogant asshole that placed his dad in the SNF under Medi-Cal guidelines and had re-allocated his father's assets for himself. The facility isn't all Medi-Cal and relatively nice as far as SNFs go. Although, I am sure there was enough money to pay for dad to be home and pay privately for medical and custodial care. Besides the fact that the son was a real schmuck, he ignored all parking lot protocol and insisted on parking his Ferrari in an undesignated parking spot when visiting his father. My buddy gave the guy one warning. One. The next time my buddy had the Ferrari towed.

If not apparent to you I was indeed developing a passion for my new career. I was still learning and I had much more information on its way. I was a real sponge. I understood that at least in terms of volume the greatest amount of potential referrals would come out of a rehabilitation setting. A few more months into the job and I was in the most north part of my territory. I was wandering around a hospital and found the office of the Director of Rehab. The gentleman in the position was named Ron Lyder.

I would say Ron was in his late thirties or maybe early forties. From the pictures in the office he was a young family man. He was nicely dressed, handsome and had an air of confidence. He seemed approachable to me. Not that it mattered. I was going to approach him anyway.

I saw Ron in his office and said, "Hi. I'm Jessica Solomon. I work for a senior care company. May I talk to you for a minute?

He reluctantly said, "Ok. Have a seat."

I proceeded to give Ron my pitch. He asked a few questions and I fired back the answers. As I was talking to him he was typing in my contact information at a faster than average speed. The guy was a real multi-tasker. His questions and composure was fast paced and he didn't seem like he really had more than a few minutes for me.

Ron said, "I am super busy and should also tell you that I won't be in this position much longer. I am moving up north. I did take down all your contact info and just sent an email blast to all contacts that should be aware of your services. I appreciate your visit and I have to go to a meeting now."

I stood up and shook Ron's hand and I said, "Thank you for your time. I really appreciate that you forwarded my information."

Ron said, "Jessica. You are going to do really well."

I said, "Really? Why?"

Ron said, "No one ever comes in my office like you just did."

I said, "What do you mean? People don't come to your office and try to meet you and visit with you?"

Ron said, "No one like you that sells the services that you are trying to sell. I wish you luck, but you won't need it.

Well, that was pretty awesome. I felt pretty good after that. I needed to have that little ego boost because I was about to visit an Assisted Living community around the corner that had coordinated a networking meeting for contacts in my industry. I would have to stand up in a room full of people which was very intimidating to me. One on one I was a rock star, but at the time I needed to overcome my fears about public speaking.

I went to the networking meeting. I did okay for a newbie. I survived. The real blessings of that meeting were meeting Mona and Dina. Mona was the Sales Director of the Assisted Living community and Dina was her boss. Dina was the Executive Director. Dina has a medical background and she knows her stuff. After the meeting was over Dina personally introduced herself to me and invited me to sit on a bench outside the conference room with her. Dina gave me the greatest career advice that I ever received and I will be forever grateful.

Dina said, "Ok. Tell me what you got here. Tell me what you are selling."

I gave my little speech to Dina. I was still riding my high from my meeting with Ron and the fact that I did not die of embarrassment of having to speak in public.

Dina smirked at me and said, "Jessica you are going to do really well in this industry. As a matter of fact you are going to do great, but you need to remember one thing. You need to remember what you are here in this industry to do. You are here to help. As long as you stay focused on what you are here to do you will be successful. Don't lose focus and don't be greedy. This industry is about helping people and don't ever forget that."

Dina was so right. I always stay true to that. There are times that the business side takes over. It has to. This is a business. Greed and competitiveness will try to find their way in, but as long as you stay true to being helpful, you can't go wrong. I share Dina's words with my colleagues and friends whenever appropriate. It's great advice.

Meeting Mona was great as well. Mona is a real lethal weapon. Very cool, confident and determined. Mona is extremely smart. I am convinced, as well as many others, that Mona can do just about anything she sets her mind to. In addition to having experience in sales, Mona also had a past career in teaching and she is a true entrepreneur at heart. We became good friends and I learned a lot from her.

It's not what Mona says that is so impactful and effective, it's the way she says it. Mona would say things like, "Fish where the fish are." and "You know sales. It's follow-up, follow-up, follow-up". It's true, true, true. We have all heard those sayings it's just when Mona says it, it strikes a chord. She also says, "No one picks my boss, I pick my boss." That's true, too. When Dina left their same employer, Mona chose to leave as well.

One of the things that are most impressive about Mona is her method of re-directing people. Mona has a real gift for making people realize what a complete and total moron they are. I once overheard her on the phone talking to a customer service representative regarding a couch that she ordered. It sounded something like this;

Mona: Okay, so what you are telling me is that you confirmed that I ordered the couch over a month ago and it's not here, correct? So, what you are telling me is that based on my purchase date the couch should be here, correct? So, what you are telling me is that I should probably cancel my order and you should refund my money? So, shouldn't I be receiving a discount due to this huge, huge, huge inconvenience to my family? So, what are you telling me?"

I call it the "Mona – so what you are telling me" method. I don't know exactly how she does it, but it is a highly effective approach and one I could never master. I have seen her do this approach a ton of times with always a successful outcome in her favor. Although, I can't do myself, I am really entertained watching Mona. She is one of my all-time favorite sales mentors.

CHAPTER 11 – MY PEGS

In one of my first months out in the field I went to a senior fair which was held at a community recreation center. My company had a booth there. The fair was filled with vendors, services, and information that catered to the senior population. It is there that I met Peggy. I like to call her Peggers.

Peggy is a special kind of people. Many would agree that she is the closest thing to an angel on earth without the angel wings. She is one of the most genuine people you will ever meet. She is the kind of woman that cream colored clothes and pearl jewelry was made for. Peggy is somewhat reserved, gentle, and just super sweet. She is a great listener and is the epitamy of love and compassion.

Peggy owns and operates a Free Placement agency for Seniors. In a nut shell, she helps people find places to live other than their own homes. Placement agencies help people find the best place for an elderly person that require assistance. Generally people that will be placed in some type of Residential care facility for the elderly (RCFE). A RCFE could be an independent or an active senior community with some assisted living component. Most of the time people need help finding placement for a family member that has dementia. They are often placed in a six bed or twelve bed RCFE. It's generally a converted home that is modified to accommodate the frail and demented population.

People will often ask how a placement agency could be free? Well, it's free to the people that are in need of the service. It's a free service for the people and families that are seeking placement. How do they make money then?... Good question.

They generate revenue by contracting with the facilities that they refer people to. The placement agency contracts with a RCFE and when a person is placed there the placement agency gets a referral fee. The amount of the fee is dependent on the fee agreed upon in the contract.

A not so obvious question that I think most people would ask is about the RCFEs that a particular placement agency is not contracted with. How can you be certain that the Placement Agency would make you aware of all options? After all, why would a placement agency refer you to a RCFE that they don't have a contract with? They wouldn't get a referral fee. Well, that's one of the bullshit things about this industry that you should know about. At the end of the day, all the information is out there and accessible to you. If you rely on your immediate source, whether good or bad, that's your deal.

That's part of the mystery here. What you don't know is what you don't know. There are lots of placement agencies out there. Some good, some bad and that's that. It's your choice if you want to work with them and it's like using any other product or services and it totally comes down to buyer beware. There are lots of national and local placement agencies that are in my opinion, bullshit. They are selective and do not give you all the information that could be available to you. They deliberately keep information from you so that they can get their referral fee.

Peggers does not work that way. As a matter of fact she gives you ALL the information and options that you can possibly choose from. I think that's another reason for her success, besides the fact that she is downright lovely, she is very honest and is here to help. Pegs gives you a list and every option available to you and then helps you narrow down the list based on preference such as location, costs, and levels of need. She will refer to a RCFE that she may not have a contract with as well. It comes down to what is best for the client.

I believed in Peggy and her business and I supported her in every way I could. I could sell her business better than home care in a New York minute. It's an easy sell and one that I took full advantage of in a good way, of course. I met with Peggy and realized forming an alliance with her would be a good idea for many reasons. She was genuine, had a great service, her service complimented our services and I also knew a free placement agency would always generate more referrals and leads than me, so I could take the leads she got that might be more interested in home care and not really interested in or ready for placement.

I suggested to Peggy that we market together and she was agreeable to that. Spending a day in the field alone can be somewhat lonely sometimes. Spending a day in the field with someone you don't really enjoy is enough to make you drive your car off a cliff. Spending the day with Peggy was synergetic, productive and downright fun. Peggy is somewhat conservative and reserved. She's a good Catholic girl with a spiritual down to earth twist.

I tried to keep a softened approach with her and respect her religious background. I don't know what the hell my problem is but when I spend time with someone that is somewhat conservative or religious, I suddenly develop Tourette's syndrome and I start cursing like a drunken sailor. I think that I am so paranoid about it that I can't help myself and I curse more than I usually would and I start dropping F-bombs all over the place.

One of the first days Peggy and I spent with each other

was in a random isolated town about an hour and a half north of the city that our offices are based in. We had a day of planned meetings and visits. We had a productive lunch with some contacts at a hospital and then Peggy suggested that we go get a coffee or something sweet. Peggy loves to eat something sweet after a meal. We went to a coffee shop, ordered our 400 calorie specialty drinks and then the day turned into another direction. That day will always be remembered as the "Mocha Crisis Day".

We started driving to our next appointment which was at a SNF. A few minutes into the drive we started to feel weird. We arrived at our appointment and waited in the lobby for our contact. We both walked over to a salt water fish tank and started to observe the fish. We were totally hypnotized by the fish. Especially one in particular that was rather large, had a face like a horse, and white milky eyes. We were staring at the fish and then a staff member noticed our observation and indicated that the fish had cataracts. My thoughts were – Really? Unbelievable. Pegs and I turned to each other and then we got dizzy.

I said, "Peggers, I don't feel too well".

Peggers said, "Jester, I don't feel well either."

We pulled it together for the meeting, but we were in a haze for the rest of the day. I am not sure how we made it back because we were sweating and on the verge of puking in the car on our way back home. We vowed to never have another mocha coffee at that coffee place ever again. It was brutal.

Now one of the things that I love about Pegs is that she thinks I am hilarious. I love recognition for my sense of humor and Pegs is one of my best audiences. When I go on a full on rampage about something Pegs always responds with, "Oh, you're a beauty." Most of the time I just make her laugh and I love to hear her chuckle. She always says, "You are so damn funny." Pegs lights up my life.

On one day of marketing Pegs and I visited a Senior Center. We sat at a table with the seniors and the Executive Director and just had a good chat and time. There was one gentleman that was sitting at the table with us. His name was Benny. Benny was blind. His eyes were the lightest blue. He was so incredibly sweet and funny. He was Jewish and originally from New York, like me. I just instantly connected with Benny. He told me that he loved to listen to classical music. I had some classical music CDs that my company had created and I went and retrieved a CD from my car to give to him. Benny was so appreciative. I was really touched by him.

As Peggy and I went to leave and say goodbye to the Executive Director I started to cry. The Executive Director said, "Benny makes me cry, too."

As Pegs and I walked to my car Pegs said, "Jester, are you okay? Are you going to be alright?"

I needed a moment to compose myself. I was just so affected by Benny and I just felt helpless. I wanted to do something for him and help him in any way I could. I also have a super weak spot for the blind. There are few things I fear in life, but the thing I fear the most is losing my eyesight. I fear that more than anything. I have so much respect for the blind and I do believe future advancements in technology will not only save diminishing eyesight, but will also cure the blind. Those technologies, unfortunately, are not available today.

About a week or two later I was in my office and I was

following up on some past leads and inquiries. We often do this to see if there is an opportunity for business, but regardless we reach out to people in need of help. Inquiring is just half the battle sometimes. Sometimes people are afraid to make decisions or make wrong decisions. It's important to follow-up no matter what just to make sure people either found a solution or a resource that they are comfortable with. Whether our company or not, people still need help and support.

I made a phone call to an adult child that was inquiring about possible services for her father. As the phone was ringing and I was reviewing the notes from the initial call I realized I was calling Benny's daughter. Benny's name was in the database and from the location of the city and the notes I knew that it had to be the same man.

I started talking to the daughter and said, "I think I met your Dad recently at the senior center."

The daughter replied, "Oh, you are the girl from the senior care company. You are that Jessica. My father told me about you."

I said, "Yes. Your father is darling. He really touched me. He is so sweet."

The daughter replied, "Oh, thank you. That is very nice. I am glad you had a nice visit. You see, the truth is that my father is a miserable man and he drives me and my sister crazy. He is absolutely cruel and mean and he is intolerable. You have no idea what he does to us. I know that you think that I am probably a terrible person for saying this. I realize my father is different to the outside world and many people adore him, but he is terrible to my sister and me and he has been our whole lives. Regardless, we do whatever we can to help him, but he refuses to cooperate. There is nothing we can really do to help him. He won't let us and he is just so cruel to us."

Needless to say, I was shocked. My whole world got turned upside down. I continued to listen to the daughter and the horror of a story she told me about not so sweet Benny. I felt really bad for her and her sister. When the call was over I felt like I was going to get in my car and go drive to Benny and tell him what an asshole he was to his kids. That's the thing you learn, though. Emotional dynamics with family members. It is what it is. You help where you can and sometimes you can help and assist with healing in many ways. Sometimes, there is years of neglect and anger and it takes tons of therapy and nurturing to break down those thick walls.

I immediately called Pegs and she answered, "What's up Jester?"

I said, "Peggers, remember Benny at the senior center?

Pegs said, "Of course, you got upset about him."

I said, "Yeah, well I just got off the phone with his daughter and apparently Benny is a real son of a bitch. So, that's it. We can have big hearts and care for people, but we are not going to cry and we are not going to get emotionally attached. We don't know the whole story. We could end up feeling bad for a real asshole."

Pegs chuckled and said, "Oh…….. You're a beauty."

CHAPTER 12 – I DID IT MY WAY

One of the things I loved about my job is that I worked for such an innovative company. From upper management down to the end user our company was always eager to improve our model and be the best we could be. The company and especially upper management were always eager to hear new ideas. A lot of ideas that I had and my colleagues shared were often implemented. It gave me motivation to be even more creative.

Janey was always open to ideas and she herself has some good ones, too. She would often say something that would point me in a new challenging direction and that's what a good hunter needs. Janey was also great in the way, like Mitch, that she let me be me. Janey let me fly from the nest very early and she really gave me the independence that someone like me requires to stay enthusiastic about my job. I often joked that I could be in Cabo sipping cocktails with my thumb up my butt and Janey wouldn't know otherwise. She really didn't know where I was or what I was doing half the time, but she didn't need to. I was always doing my job and I was doing it well.

One of our company's objectives was to help one client at a time. Sounds good. Sounds like what people want and need. Sounds like a very customized and individualized approach for the end-user and that's what our company wanted to do. Well, that sounds great, but Jessica Solomon wanted many clients, as many as possible, all at one time. The model of our company really supported individuals in their own place of residence. I saw the potential to support supplemental care giving in senior communities and facilities. Not just supplemental care for the actual patients and residents, but for the facilities to utilize our company if they did not have enough staff. It wasn't really what our model was supporting, because then we would be just a staffing agency. Other guidelines have to be followed and they didn't want the reputation or headache of being a staffing agency.

Here is another example of being at the right place at the right time. I was at the main hospital in my town and I was trying to connect with the Director of Discharge Planning. These days I don't even know if I have the energy or the lack of knowledge to attempt something so dangerous. The Director was not that nice of a lady. Okay, she was kind of a bitch. I can understand because you have to be bitchy in that position sometimes. She needs to do her job. Getting solicited by vendors is rather distracting and downright annoying.

To this day, I can't even remember what the hell I did that pissed her off. I am not sure if she replied to an email that I had forwarded to her and her team or she sent me an email that copied her team, but it was nasty and she made me look like an idiot. Well, just so you know, Jessica Solomon doesn't go down like that. If she had a beef with me, that's fine. I can take that, and try to do my best to diffuse it. However, she copied other innocent individuals and that I will not tolerate. I immediately fired back an email that was creatively coded in such a way that I not only asked for forgiveness, but I outlined what a moron and miserable bitch she was. Believe me, it was creatively written because she responded with an apology and invited me to meet with her in her office.

So, I met with Ms. Balls to the Wall and we had a great conversation. I always can seem to find a common ground with anybody. Turns out from the photos in her office she was a Harley

Davidson chick. Who would have ever thought? Well, I really earned her respect when I told her that I used to ride on the bitchpad of my ex-boyfriend's Harley. I excluded the part about how you would never get me on another motorcycle ever again.

Ms. Balls said that there wasn't a whole lot she thought she could do for me, but she walked me down the hall to the Director of Patient Services, Felicia. I had a nice chat with Felicia and she led me across the hall to the nurse staffing department where she was going to introduce me to Annie. Annie wasn't there at the moment, but we decided to set a meeting to further discuss the possibilities of my company doing supplemental staffing for the hospital.

It was time to call in the big guns. I was already learning how to utilize Janey. When I was working with a family that had unrealistic high expectations and lived in a delusional ego-centric world, I would send Janey out to meet with them. This was usually in cases with the severely wealthy who are sometimes more about aesthetics and image than anything else. It's not that the other Care Managers didn't cut the mustard, but Janey happens to have an appearance and disposition that makes people think that they are in the hands of an upper class professional.

Janey also has a medical background and if I wanted this deal to go down with the hospital, I was going to have to bring in someone that spoke their language. I also would need Janey's support to pull this off and sell the idea to our own company. It's not really what our model was about, but it seemed like there was some serious revenue potential. I also kept hearing my father's words in my head –*Jess, don't go apeshit.* I was totally going to go apeshit, but I would be way more composed with Janey as my co-pilot.

Janey and I met with Annie and we moved forward with a contract with the hospital. Our caregivers were only staffed for companion care. They could not have any patient contact. They were there to monitor impulsive patients or extremely agitated patients. If the patients required any medical assistance or support our caregivers were to alert the hospital staff. It started out rocky, but in a few weeks it was smooth sailing.

Although my company had some reservations I think in the end they were pleased. That "account" generated over six hundred thousand dollars in about a year and a half. Oh, it gets better. Since we had care givers on most of the floors and on most days patients would inquire about our services because our care givers were wearing shirts and name tags with our company logos. Also, hospital staff was getting used to seeing us and would also refer us to patients and families seeking home care services. We generated additional business as a result from just having a presence in the hospital.

That hospital was without a CFO and CEO almost during the whole time we were riding the gravy train. The hospital nursing staff really took advantage of utilizing our services because it made their jobs easier due to the fact that they had an extension of their staff to monitor some of the more difficult patients. The nurse staffing department said that we were the first company that they ever utilized like that. It really did come down to being at the right place at the right time.

The gravy train came to a halt. The hospital had hired a CFO and CEO and I think that they themselves were almost admitted to the hospital when they saw the money that was going to my company. They immediately pulled together a team to hire and train their own employees to do the same tasks at about half the rate that they were being charged by us. Hey, it was really fun while it lasted.

Another creative direction Janey sent me in was to go to the Indian reservation about thirty minutes north of our office. Native Americans? Sure, I'll give it a whirl. Sounds like an adventure to me. I'm an Aries. I do love adventure. One of our office members was somehow connected to one of the Elders on the reservation so I called and set an appointment.

I approached one of the many mobiles homes on the reservation. There was one mobile home after the other all lined up with their obvious love for Chevy trucks. I entered the home of the Elder and it was interesting to say the least. There must have been walls somewhere in the home, but it was difficult to know for sure. There were knick knacks lined up and piled up from floor to ceiling. I don't remember being offered a chair to sit in, but I also don't remember seeing one either.

I was taken on a tour of the backyard. When you were in the backyard you thought you were on another planet. It was beautiful and spacious and the Elder brought me over to where the sweat lodge is assembled. The Elder explained how they use the sweat lodge for ceremonies and rituals. They have drumming, prayers and offerings to the spirit world. Inside the lodge you are naked and you can go to sweat lodges with men and women or if you prefer then you can attend one that has all the same sex.

The Elder said, "Would you like to come to a sweat lodge? You may have to stand outside several times before you are invited in the lodge."

I was still stuck on the naked part and said, "Did you say that you have to be naked?'

The Elder replied, "Yes."

I said, "Sounds tempting. I'll have to think about it."

While the Elder and I was outside there was a younger man that was walking around the house and the yard. He was loading and unloading things. If I had to gage the age difference between the Elder and the young man, I'd say a good hundred years. I assumed he was helping with yard work. I didn't give much thought to what their relationship was or how they were related.

The Elder and I drove up to the Health Center on the reservation and she walked me into a conference room. She left me in the room by myself to see if she could find some contacts for me to speak with and exchange information. The Elder returned and we continued to have a conversation about the reservation and the health center. Then the Elder started to talk about the young man I saw in her yard.

The Elder said, "I had no intentions of ever marrying again. I had absolutely no interest at all. But then my husband (the young man in the yard) would not stop pursuing me. He was very adamant. My uncle that passed over many years ago still speaks to me from the spirit world and he told me that this man is a good man and you should marry him. He will be good to you and provide security and a good future. So I married him."

Huh. Interesting. I couldn't help myself and said, "is there any chance the next time you talk to your uncle you can mention Jessica Solomon and see what he says about a man in my future?'

CHAPTER 13 – OH BABY, BABY IT'S A WILD WORLD

It didn't take much time and I was feeling like a pro. Now that I had been gaining experience and having more conversations with referral sources and adult children I was able to "seal the deal" with much more ease. It was after Thanksgiving and we were now approaching the Christmas holiday. Sometimes there is no rhyme or reason on how busy or slow this industry can be. Sometimes it's all about the season.

Depending on several circumstances it is a tough call to bring a loved one home back from a SNF setting. There is a lot of apprehension for family members, especially if they are not in the local area. This is an area where our kind of company really shines because we have enough layers of oversight and expertise to help relatives care for their loved ones from afar.

I was visiting a SNF and there was a woman who was rather obstinate about her rehab treatment. She was still sharp. She had her mental faculties. This woman sat upright in a chair with her pen and pad and her notes and would not let go of the facility's portable phone. She really wanted out of there. So much so that she refused treatment. This woman would probably do much better with one on one care in the home and she did have the resources to pay for care.

Although she could probably coordinate a return to her home by herself if she really was persistent enough, her son was the obstacle. The son lived about three hours away and he was too nervous to let his mother go home with care. I had several conversations with the son and it came down to the fact that he had to give his approval, but he just could not pull the trigger. This was what my fifth call to the son sounded like...

Me: I hate to create a sense of urgency, (that's exactly how I do create it) but we are rapidly approaching the Christmas holiday and then we are going to get into a scheduling frenzy with all the other clients that want care around the holiday. You should really consider making a decision as soon as possible.

Son: I'm just not sure that is best from my mother.

Me: Why?

Son: I am so far away from her.

Me: Did I thoroughly explain the model of our company to you? You should feel confident that we could manage your mother's care and update you frequently. The physical therapists at the facility have given up on treatment since your mother refuses it. She agreed that she would be more compliant in her own home with physical therapy services.

Son: I know, but I am afraid it won't go well.

Me: It's not going well right now. At least you have a better shot of her getting stronger and being happier in her own home.

Son: I know, but she might end up getting sick and then returning to the hospital.

Me: LISTEN, your mother has enough resources to go back home. She doesn't want to be in a hospital. If she wants to go home and still refuses treatment, at least she is in her own home. If you were in a hospital on Christmas, but you could go home, where would you want to be?

Son: You are right. Please make arrangements for my mother to return home.

Here's the sucky part. We got so incredibly busy that we couldn't arrange discharge for another three days or after that upcoming weekend. It was a rare occasion, but we were getting absolutely slammed. Also, after we spoke to the woman and let her know that her son agreed to let her return home, she herself was apprehensive. Go figure. The woman did eventually return home and she did quite well with services and was compliant with her therapies. And to all a good night!

It was a week before Christmas and there was an influx of requests coming in. Honey Bunny called with three or more referrals that wanted to be home for the holiday. He asked if I would meet with a few families that were interviewing home care companies and I immediately came to the facility. I walked in and Honey Bunny immediately started guiding me to the patient rooms with family members. He said, "I'll line 'em up (as he smacked his hands together) and you knock 'em down." LOVED Honey Bunny, loved!

I needed some backup. I called Janey and a Care Manager. They came down to the facility and started to coordinate the paperwork for the families. Honey Bunny and I would hang out in the office and when we saw them leave a room we would be waiting to point to another room and then they had to talk to another inquiry. Janey and the Care Manager were getting totally exhausted. Honey Bunny and I sat in the Physical Therapy room and ate some of his birthday cake from earlier in the day. I clearly had the position in the company that had the most fun.

I would often visit Norma in her new home, the memory

care unit in a beautiful Assisted Living community. Norma was the first client I ever met of my company. She would always remain my favorite client. We continued to provide supplemental services and would take Norma off campus for social outings. I would love to see her and her smiling face. Norma is also really good for the ego.

I would walk up to Norma and hold her hands when I spoke to her. I'd say, "Hi Norma, you look so pretty today."

Norma didn't know who I was, but always responded with, "How are you? I am so glad to see you. Why haven't you come to visit me?

I responded with, "I'm visiting you now."

Then out came the heavy compliments. Norma always asked, "Are you married?"

I said, "No."

Norma then said, "Why aren't you married? I can't believe you are not married. You are so beautiful."

Oh, Norma. She was always a great ego-booster. I was getting worried about her, though. She looked really happy and healthy, but she put on a lot of weight. I was wondering if it had anything to do with medication. I asked Patty if she had visited with Norma lately, and if she had noticed her weight gain. Patty thought it was due to the fact that Norma was eating really well and may be eating too much. Patty also thought that Norma was not getting enough exercise in her new home. Norma was now in a group setting so she now got less one on one interaction and attention.

I wasn't too happy with the fact that Norma might not be getting enough attention, but she looked happy. She was safe in her new environment. I visited Norma just about every time I was in her area.

CHAPTER 14 – THE DEVIL REALLY DOES WEAR PRADA

In a short period of time I ramped up relatively quickly. The bigger challenges about life, love, and business were still ahead of me. I was a little more than a year into my job and at that time I got involved in a romantic relationship. Well, it started out romantic. What you see is not always what you get. I stayed in a very unhealthy and volatile relationship for the next three years. The poison in my personal life seeped into my professional life on some levels. It was hard to separate at times, because my significant other also worked for the same employer. That's all I have to say about that.

I learned just how much I should never judge a book by its cover. You shouldn't either. What seems like a crystal palace, a secure environment or a genuine person could just be smoke and mirrors. Sometimes when something looks appealing and presents itself with everything you could have imagined and more, you have to consider the possibility that it may be too good to be true. I have seen pure evil at work and it's not pretty at all.

When you look for an employer do you look at the status of the position offered and also the benefit and compensation package or do you consider the people you will be working with and how much you will enjoy what you do for a living every day? When you look for a partner does it matter what they look like on the outside or do you care more about what is in the inside? When choosing a facility or senior community for a loved one are you in search of a pretty environment with plenty of amenities or are you more concerned about the quality of care and how genuinely happy your loved one will be?

The questions I pose are not one dimensional and either are the answers. There are certainly many variables and options to consider. The thing I want to stress is to know what all your options truly are and when you make a decision, you should be as comfortable as you possibly can be with that decision. Senior care and health care in general all involves people. I have seen some of the most genuine people with the biggest hearts you could ever meet. I have seen wonderful people with the best intentions make careless decisions. I've seen some heartless people commit heartless acts.

You just might enter a SNF with marble floors and wall papered walls. It might be the cleanest facility you have ever seen and would think to yourself that you could eat off the clean floors if you had to. You might enjoy seeing polished silver and glass chandeliers. You might be tempted to walk in the lush and colorful center courtyard. You might see the pint size owner administrator wearing her designer clothes and the fact that she is totally oblivious that she has a strong need to fire her horrid personal shopper.

What you might not see when you visit that facility is a woman in a wheel chair in her room. You might not see the woman who uncontrollably trembles and shakes due to her debilitating Parkinson's disease. You might not see this woman who has no family to advocate for her. You might not see her do her favorite thing in the world which is to use the hand rails around the facility and walk as much as she can. You might not see her because she may be in a room that that has her bed positioned so that she is unable to leave her room or wheelchair. You might not see her because the administrator doesn't like the way she looks when people visit the facility.

People and places might present one way, but it's what's in the inside that really matters. I am not a regulator by any means, but I can get a general idea of how well some place is managed within minutes. It comes down to who is managing it. It always starts at the top. Whether that means the administrator, owner, or corporation that is running the show that is how the rest of the business operates. Usually, you can really get the best reading on how a business operates by looking at the employees. They are the facilitators of the organization. If they are happy and upbeat, then you are headed in the right direction.

In terms of the geriatric population when a patient is admitted to the hospital that facility is looking for a three day turn around. Most people will require additional tests, rest and rehabilitation. Due to money and medical reimbursement the majority of those patients will go to a SNF. They generally need that additional care and the hospital has to make sure that they are covering all bases and have a safe patient discharge.

Upon discharge from a SNF that facility has to make sure that they have a safe discharge, too. If the client requires a certain level of care that exceeds a few hours they are generally going to be referred to a RCFE. I was looking for the patients that do not want to go to a RCFE. I was seeking to provide the custodial services if they are in need of them if they return to their own residence. The other thing that I provided for discharges from a SNF is assistance with a safe discharge plan. Regulatory agencies will monitor if patients are continually admitted to an Emergency room or to a SNF. Re-admits are not good for facilities. Especially, if the patients are re-admitted for the same condition.

I was once speaking to a director of several SNFs. I asked, "So, do you have any frequent flyers (patients that are re-admitted)?

The director replied, "I hope so".

I was confused. I said, "Isn't that bad if they are re-admitted?"

He said, "Depends on what they are re-admitted for. After they leave here from a broken hip, I'd like them to come back with the other broken hip. And then a broken arm and then a broken leg. I want them to come back with every broken limb."

Whoa. That's morbid. I couldn't handle the truth. However, that's a business component to this industry. I had to stop and think about what I was seeking. I know I don't want anyone in pain and suffering. I know how sad I was when I thought about the people that do require some form of assistance. I got back to focusing on what I thought to be true. My company, like any other similar company, had its challenges, but at the end of the day, we did it the best. If someone was going to need assistance, they might as well hire the best company to help them. It was my job to let the end-user and their personal contacts know that we were an option.

CHAPTER 15 – LEAN ON ME

I have heard that when people fall in love and stay together for a long time the years just start melting into each other. The year that usually always stays fresh in their minds was their first year together. I remember more stories about my days in the field and the clients that I met in my first year in senior care than any other year.

I made some great friends over the next few years. Senior care is such an incestuous industry. People are constantly jumping between different companies and senior communities. It's also another good reason to never burn your bridges. As a matter of fact, one of my strategies was to help recruit people I had strong relationships with when I learned about open job positions.

One time I knew of a senior community in need of a Director of Assisted Living. My friend, Jo-Ann, was debating if she actually wanted to apply for the position. I knew my friend was a valuable commodity and I encouraged her to at least interview for the position. The bigger picture was that I would be placing a good contact in a position that would potentially drive more business for me. I knew I could help connect Jo-Ann to the Executive Director, Bill. Jo gave me the green light.

I called Bill and said, "Bill, did you hire anyone for the open position, yet?"

Mind you, this is about 4:45pm on a Friday.

Bill replied, "As a matter of fact, I am standing over the fax machine and ready to send the paperwork to corporate to make an offer to an applicant."

I said, "Put the fax down and step away from the machine! I got your girl."

Jo-Ann was hired shortly after. She did a terrific job. I did get some leads and I was totally appreciative of them. However, the level of acuity in the community decreased. I got leads when appropriate, but placing Jo-Ann in that position actually had an adverse effect on creating more potential clients from that community. Jo-Ann really worked those care givers to support the residents. She made the residents get more exercise. That campus became livelier and healthier do to Jo-Ann's passion for good health. That's just another great example why the right management is so important.

Peggy and I bonded more. I am not a big red meat eater. I generally don't eat it and it has been phased out of my diet for several years now. Except for when I go out with Peggers. We always get together for a steak dinner about once every three months. One of the first times we went out for dinner she was constantly getting interrupted with calls from her sisters. Pegs is one of nine children. Pegs is the baby in the family.

For such a big family that is spread so wide they are pretty close and well connected. Pegs was trying to keep it together. She had to shut the phone off after a while. Both of Peggy's parents were actively dying and the family was keeping every one updated. Talk about actively dying, though. Seriously, her parents were touch and go for the next two years. They would be just on the verge of passing and then out of nowhere they would recover and remain stable until the next crisis.

Poor Pegs. She was constantly going back and forth to the

Palm desert which is about five hours from her home. I offered to go with her any time she didn't want to go alone, but she made the trip solo time and time again. After a long struggle and time her parents passed away. They passed away within months of each other. Shortly after Pegs and I went out for dinner and I noticed a beautiful ring on her finger. It belonged to her mother. Her sisters and she decided that they would rotate the ring around the daughters every year. I hope her sisters decide to let Peggy keep the ring with her always. I know she misses her mother terribly.

My company had made the decision to expand our territory. They wanted to service the next county north of us. I really embraced the challenge to open up a new market. In a relatively short period of time we ramped up the market in the northern territory. I had so much fun doing it. It was such a beautiful area to market in and I would stay in a hotel for a few nights at a time so I got to be part of the community. I made some wonderful friends and it almost felt more like vacation than work. Well, not all the time.

We had started new services for a client that was in the late stages of dementia. This woman, Millie, had been living alone, but had family that was nearby that were very loving and supportive. Both Millie's mind and body was rapidly declining. She required around the clock care and supervision. Besides the obvious there was also another reason why Millie required 24 hour supervision. Millie required protection from someone that was financially abusing her.

You got to think what kind of sick and pathetic individual would prey on someone so frail and defenseless? You got to wonder how a relatively young gentleman would take advantage of such a sick and troubled woman? It must be perplexing that someone would take the time to convince this demented and helpless woman that she was someone in a romantic relationship with this sick twisted lowlife. It must be downright mind blowing to learn that this piece of shit was also an active employee of the local law enforcement.

I had just got done with a long day of marketing and I was ready to retire to my hotel room. I received a phone call from the Care Manager that was overseeing Millie's case. The Care Manager informed me that Millie had been extremely agitated that day and as of lately had been ejecting herself from her wheel chair and throwing temper tantrums. She was becoming a real danger to herself. The Care Manager indicated that Millie was still very agitated and that the current care giver, which was new to the client case, needed some additional support. Due to her current eye procedure, the Care Manager could not drive in the dark and she asked me if I would be able to go visit with the care giver and client.

My first thought – No. Second thought - No way. Third thought - No can do. I was in a tough spot. I absolutely adored the Care Manager and I wanted to support her in every way I could, but I think what she was asking me to do was beyond my scope of practice. The Care Manager indicated that the care giver was very uneasy about being alone with the client and it was more about making sure the care giver had a witness should Millie really hurt herself. The Care Manager said that there was a call out to the family and the neurologist and everybody was on standby to see if Millie would stabilize.

Okay, so I decided to take one for the team. I followed the Care Manager's directions and instructions. I was to make a very smooth entrance. No doorbell or knocking. The care giver knew when I had arrived and had the door open for me. Millie was in her wheelchair and close to the door. The care giver looked relieved that someone had arrived, but I think that she was exhausted from being with Millie and would have preferred another care giver to relieve her from her shift.

I am an educated woman. I have learned a lot about the senior care industry and dementia. But seriously, I think the care giver thought I was a moron for sure. I would try to converse with Millie, but that was too stimulating for her. I was just trying to calm her down. She was really upset. So, in addition to this poor care giver having to decompress Millie, she had to re-direct me as well. She constantly shook her head at me and would say, "shhhhhh."

Millie was originally from England. The care giver had put on a DVD from an old British sitcom and that usually put Millie at ease. Although, this time it wasn't working. I went over to Millie's bookshelves. I saw a plethora of great books. I absolutely adore Princess Diana and I could go through books of pictures of her and the royal family for days. I grabbed a book and sat down next to Millie. I started to turn the pages in front of her.

Millie would point to the photos and say, "That is Princess Diana. That is Prince Charles. That is the Queen Mother."

I was thinking, hey, maybe I do know what I am doing after all. Millie had calmed down quite a bit. It's like I always say, I can always find a common ground with just about anyone. Millie and I were both fond of the royal family. We could look at books for hours. Piece of cake.

Then Millie looked at me with such a tremendous amount

of terror in her face. Millie started weeping and said, "Please let me go. Please, please, please. I won't tell anyone. I promise. I swear." She started sobbing uncontrollably and said, "Please. I just want my babies. Please bring me my babies. I want to be with my children. Please don't take my children away. I want to be with my daughter. Please. I am begging you."

Okay, so picture book time was over. I thought Millie and I were connecting, but apparently I misjudged. The care giver continued to coordinate calls with the neurologist who was directing the care giver to give a specific medication to Millie, but she would refuse it. The care giver had to tell the daughter to come to Millie's home. At this point, it was the only thing we could do. Millie still recognized her daughter and would be relieved to see her.

Before the daughter's arrival, Millie became quite agitated. She went into full on demon mode and boy, if looks could kill I would have died right on the spot. She told me everything she thought I did and I was going to pay the price. She was going to make sure of it. Then the daughter arrived and as quick as she came in the door was as quick as I left. I flew out of there like a bat out of hell. Millie continued to decline and died shortly after. I am sure she is in a much more peaceful place now.

CHAPTER 16 – WE'RE ALL DYING

On one of my visits with my family I was hanging in my parents' bedroom with my mother. We were laying on the bed and chit chatting away and then we heard my father upstairs raising his voice with frustration. My father was on the phone with a business connection. My father's business connection apparently screwed up a business transaction that my father and he were working on together.

I said to my mother, "Who is dad raising his voice to?'

My mother gave a frown and replied, "Joel". My mother continued and said, "I know Joel is a putz and I can't stand that he calls ninety five times a day, but I feel so bad for him. His mother is dying and I can't believe Daddy is raising his voice at him. Do you think you could say something to Daddy? He'll probably listen to you."

Sure. I love a good intervention. I waited until my father's phone call ended. I walked out of my parent's room and into the living room. I called up to my father who was in the upstairs loft which is also a TV room and an office.

I yelled, "Dad! Dad!"

My father walked to the edge of the loft and he leaned over the wall and was in my view of sight.

I said, "Dad who are you talking to like that?'

My dad replied, "I was talking to Joel. You know what he did?"

I said, "Yeah. I know what he did, but his mother is dying."

My father had a shocked look on his face. He empathetically said, "Really? How do you know?"

I replied, "Mom told me."

My father, still stunned, said, "Joel's mother died?

I said, "No, she's DYING."

My father now realizing that he misunderstood, shrugged his shoulders, raised his arms with his open palms facing the ceiling and said, "We're all dying".

It's true. From the moment you are born you start dying. It's what you do in the in-between time that is so important. You have to take good care of yourself. Of course, when you are young you don't always think about it. When you're a kid you think it's going to be a whole millennium by the time you become an adult. You take the common risks in life like no sun block in the sun. Smoke 'em if you got 'em. Keg parties in the woods. Dancing queen late at night up in da clubs. Sleep? Sleep is for the weak. How about that fast food burger? Would you like to super-size that? How about that vodka cocktail? Less tonic? Less ice? Screw it, just set up an I.V. so the liquor hits quicker. Why drink water when you have an endless amount of options of flavored drinks to poison your body?

Oh boy, it gives new meaning to the phrase, 'youth is wasted on the young'. You don't quite get the meaning until you are on the other side of young. No one anticipated people would live as long as they do now. It doesn't take a financial genius to figure out why Social Security is being depleted. Why is there such an influx of people that have Alzheimer's disease? You know why, because people are living longer mostly due to the fact that there are all these medications that keep their bodies going, but we have not got grip on the meds that will fix the brain part.

So now what we have is a high rate of people that will live for years. Well, their bodies will, but their minds won't. Not unless technology advances are made or if people would actually take into consideration that they have to actually start taking better care of themselves. It wasn't until the 1960's, when partially due to John F. Kennedy's presidency, that there was more awareness on how important exercise is for the body. More awareness on nutrition followed later.

In every city or town you will find local gyms and exercise centers. You know what is coming to a town near you? What we will probably see in the future, whether in your home or at a local center will be brain exercise centers. We have enough education and information that everyone would undeniably agree the importance of exercise for the body. Depending on what you do day to day or what you do after you retire can have an impact on what will happen to your brain. You know, your central nervous system?

However, there are no guarantees. I have seen many people with dementia that have no idea what is going on with themselves or around them. No one is really exempt. I have seen people with various prior professions, such as; civil engineers, accountants, professors, architects, blue collar workers, white collar workers, they all come from different walks of life. It's kind of like when you hear about the tri-athlete that is a pillar of health and gets struck with some obscure rare disease and suddenly dies.

Being in this industry you start to think about the things you need to do to improve your health and you often think about the people that you care about and love and you want them to take better care of themselves, too. I share what I can or until someone shuts me up. You get a new perspective on things when you see what people and other families have to go through. It can be very heartbreaking and enlightening, to say the least.

I once attended a conference that had a neurologist speaking about dementia. He explained that just because you have some memory loss it doesn't mean you are going to go through a tailspin of forgetfulness and lose all mental capacity. Memory loss is something that typically accompanies the aging process. Sometimes, a little water and some vitamin K can work wonders. Did you say your mom has totally lost it out of nowhere? Have her tested for a UTI. Sometimes it's that simple. The first rule is, don't freak out.

What I really enjoyed about the conference that I attended was the part of the presentation when a Marriage Family Therapist (MFT) spoke. The woman was kind of a combo MFT/comedian. Seriously, she does both professions and combines them for her presentations. What was so interesting is when she spoke about her elderly clients. She had an eighty six year old client who was still angry with her mother from something that happened over fifty years ago. Good grief, woman! Let it the hell go!

The MFT continued to tell stories about all these elderly clients that were hanging on to all this baggage and issues that they had a hard time resolving. I don't know what all the stories were and maybe there were some horrific stories that she didn't share with us, but the ones she told us about seemed a little ridiculous to me. She said that the statute of limitations on the issues that you have with your parents should end between the ages of eighteen and twenty one. That's when you are an adult and you need to take some responsibility for your actions, emotions and what type of re-conditioning you seek.

Interesting. I know that my mother told me that her father, Pa, never got over the fact that he was forced to take his sister to the movies with him and his friends when he was really young. Pa was well into his seventies and he was still kind of pissed off about that. I have seen a lot of folks in need of help and there is such animosity between child and parent that the incapable parent is left to fend for them self. You wouldn't let a completely obnoxious and unmanageable child alone and let them fend for themselves? Well, besides that it is illegal, no one with good sense would leave a child alone to care for themselves.

Yet, people turn away from their families often. The lesson there is, you better be good to your family. If you can't depend on them, you better have a good plan in place, because sooner or later, someone you don't know may be making your decisions for you. Or people that don't like you very much could be part of the decision making process.

CHAPTER 17 – SOCIAL WORK

My idea of Social Work is when you come home exhausted from a day of work and all you want to do is slip into a coma and you have a needy girlfriend that begs you to go out with them. The idea of getting in the shower, squeezing into your skinny clothes, and having to put on your make-up and join in on drinking festivities is grueling. You of course forget all of this after your second cocktail and in the late night cab ride home. You realize what a good friend you are after dealing with the aftermath and recovery process that ruins your whole next day. You were forced to be social which required a lot of energy that you didn't have so therefore it can be considered Social Work.

When I spoke to families that were usually in crisis mode I would collect their information, listen to their inquiries and if they were interested in learning more about my company I would connect them with a Care Manager who would then further explain their roles to the potential clients and start creating a care plan for them. I hate to say it, but the truth is, the more panicked and desperate the caller is the better. They need a solution and they need it fast. The sales cycle is very short and the chances of them engaging services are greater.

When you work in retail the customers usually come in the following types; loyal, discount, impulse, need-based and wandering. It's not that different in senior care. In general, we are dealing with need-based clients. Those types of clients have a need for our services and will incorporate some type of care plan no matter how that happens or if they even choose to work with a company. Most people assume that home care's biggest competitor is senior communities, but actually we mostly compete with family members.

There are so many reasons why families will not pull the trigger on engaging services. Many people do not see the value of incorporating a care plan because they simply do not want to spend the money. I get it. The family may not have the resources or they refuse to spend the money or there is a difference of opinion on how to spend money. Don't forget about those adult kids chomping at the bit to get their inheritance. The bummer is that when the need is great and no care plan is incorporated they usually hit a crisis and living at home may never be a feasible option ever again. Sometimes hitting some type of crisis is the catalyst people need in order to understand the need for an interdependent solution.

Sometimes you have the occasional adult child that thinks that they are making some progress for the family by just making a phone call. They call to inquire about services, ask a series of questions and then after, they feel that they have been educated on something they really did not feel like gaining an education on and their brain reaches their information threshold. They hit maximum capacity on information and they shut down. Maybe you'll hear from them again after they hit crisis mode. Their brain suddenly opens up to accept more information.

You also have the elderly themselves that could be undeniably in need of some help but they are totally resistant. I was once visiting a hospital and the Discharge Planner asked me to visit with a woman who lived alone and would be returning home. Same old story – she had neighbors and friends that help her and she does not need help. Even the fact that she woke up in a hospital with a broken hip and does not know how she got there. It's very common.

I went to visit the woman in her room that was overweight, lying on her back and using oxygen due to her COPD. It probably took over fifteen minutes for her to get herself out of bed and to the bathroom. I am being generous, it probably took her about twenty minutes.

I asked the woman, "Would you like to meet with a Care Manager?'

She replied, "No. I don't need any help."

I begged to differ. I said, "You don't need help with cooking or cleaning?'

She said, "No. I don't need any help."

I asked, "What about transportation?'

The woman replied, "No."

I then said, "What about vaccuming?" I knew I had her.

The woman raised her eyebrows when I mentioned the vacuum. I at least piqued her interest, but she was solid as a rock. She was resistant and not willing to budge. It happens.

Now the calls that really drain the hell out of me are the totally hysterical callers. The people that cry are usually very unstable. I don't mean to sound like I don't have any empathy, but I can tell you after being in the industry for over five years that people that cry are not your average callers and they will keep you on the phone for hours. They are not even always crying about their parent who needs help. They cry because of their poor relationship with their parent and most often because of major sibling rivalry.

I have had people that call me after work hours because it's more convenient for them and I soon figured out that it was their chance to pour them self a glass of wine and talk to the Elder Care Consultant for some consultation time. I guess it is fair to assume that the Elder Care Consultant is free of charge, eager to listen, and has no life of their own? I started to make sure I had other things to do just so I could give the caller a fair amount of venting time, but not to exceed to the point that I wanted to stick a fork in my eye after a good thirty minutes.

Once I was on vacation with my sister Julie, who happens to have a degree in Social Work, and she overheard me on the phone with an adult child. My sister had remarked at how she couldn't believe how I handled the call and she said that I sounded like a social worker. I was really shocked when my sister told me that because I felt like I had a limited skill set in that area and I guess I was gaining some tools whether I wanted to or not.

I was once introduced to a woman who was seeking advice and support for her mother and step-father. The woman I met was one of three sisters and she was currently unattached. She had no husband or children. She herself was having some health issues, but the worst thing she suffered from was denial. I think over the course of six months I spoke to her about fourteen times and I logged about eighteen hours of time in person and on the phone.

The woman was very elegant and poised. I was certain that her jewelry and clothes that she was wearing were worth more than three quarters of my yearly salary. She had a lot of love and sympathy for her step-father who she said suffered from narcolepsy. I believe that she diagnosed him herself and that he was just very frail and would take a lot of naps. She could not wrap her mind around her mother's problems and could not understand the intermittent signs of dementia.

After countless phone calls and listening to how she had all these underlying issues and anger towards her mother I had about all I could take. I was at the end of my rope with her. I tried referring her to the Alzheimer's Association so she could educate herself more. I was hoping that she would learn why it was that her mother was now behaving the way she was, but the daughter would only absorb the information she wanted to absorb and would try to pick things apart so it would grant an explanation that she would be more comfortable in understanding. However, it never quite worked.

I finally said, "Listen, I know that we have had the same conversation several times and we are still landing in the same spot. I and other members of my organization have spent many hours trying to assist you and come up with creative care plans for your parents. At this point, I don't think there is much else we can do unless you actually engage our services. I don't want you to take any offense to this, but I suggest that you go to your local video store and rent the movie, *The Notebook*. It may help you get some clarity."

The woman replied, "You know, you are the second person that said that to me."

Well, hello sister. There was a really good reason for that. I hate to make a generalization, but it's some of the more wealthy people that have a hard time dealing with the aging process. They live in this completely different world where money can solve a lot of problems. Unfortunately, money cannot fix or correct the debilitating effects of dementia. When you have an endless source of financial resources you can get used to throwing money at a problem to solve it. However, money does not buy you love, happiness, or a quick fix to dementia.

CHAPTER 18 – MONEY, MONEY, MONEY…..MONEY

Even though I had the attitude that my company didn't have any competition, we of course, did. I competed with families that couldn't pull the trigger. I competed with other care giving agencies which could be a mom and pop business, an independent Care Manager that outsources care giving services or the care giver underground network. There is also the occasional franchise that pops into town.

Oh, I love a good franchise. I love to meet with the newbie in town. I like to be one of their first meetings. I take a very Peggy approach to them. I actually give them all the ins and outs of the city and the contacts. I give them all the information they will ever need. I like to give them my biggest contacts. I know how loyal my referral sources are and I just give them a heads up when the newbie will be knocking on their door.

There are a few reasons why I am so generous. At the end of the day if they are going to be successful or crash and burn it will have nothing to do with me. I just like to gauge where they are coming from. If they are strong, then I want to assist them and form an alliance any way I can. If they are weak then they are on their own and it will just be a matter of time when their true colors will shine through. The proof is in the pudding. There is not a lot of in between in this industry. If you do a great job your reputation will get out there. If your business is weak, it only takes a couple of screw ups in this industry and you might as well close shop and save yourself the time.

This senior care industry is growing. Whether you took an economics class or not, you know that when demand goes up, so does the supply. From a business perspective and opportunity you can assume that this would be a good venture in some capacity to be related to senior care or health care. But here's the thing, it can't always be just about business, money and your model. It's about people. I like to take an interview approach to get to know my new competition.

I have met very charismatic and entrepreneur minded individuals. I have met developers that have built some amazing communities. I have seen independent Care Managers marketing their services like crazy. I have seen people with great expectations and I have seen them fail time and time again. They don't have the core piece of the business down. They don't understand the needs of the end-users. They aren't educated enough to understand the nature of their behaviors. They really don't understand because they don't care about that. They see this industry mostly as a business and if you are not in touch with the end users and what they need you will never make it. Also, everyone in the industry will know it and they will not support you. They may not say anything bad about you, but they won't recommend you either. That's how it works.

Let's talk about franchises, because they are coming to a town near you. They get support on the marketing components like advertising and collateral. They have standard operating procedures and like any other franchise they appear to have a national presence. It's like going to any other McDonald's in that sense. You can't really tell one from the other, yet there are different owners on a local level. Basically, it comes down to how that local franchise is being operated. Some are better than others and they generally have a good reputation.

Let's look at Mom and Pop businesses. Or not. I really

rather not look at them, but as long as we are talking about them you should know that it is totally buyer beware. Sometimes people like to go this route because they have a neighbor or friend that knows somebody that uses them. I don't want to totally knock it because there can be really good ones, but you better find out if the employees are insured and bonded. Is the business paying for workman's compensation? Are they doing the appropriate payroll taxes? What kind of screening are they conducting? Do they do criminal background checks and DMV background checks? How far back are they looking? Do they test for Tuberculosis? Do they do reference checks? Most importantly – where is their oversight? Who is watching them?

This brings us to independent Care Mangers which I have some mixed thoughts about as well. I think a lot of that has to do with the geographic location you are in and that will determined how professional and educated they really are. I think what you need to know about independent Care Managers is that there are a select few that don't have any specialized education and degree, but they consider themselves experts regarding geriatric care. Independent Care Managers typically outsource the care giving component and just so you know, they can't supervise those care givers because they are not their employees. They can only monitor the care plan that they put in place.

Here's the other thing about independent Care Managers. They generally charge about anywhere from fifty to one hundred and fifty dollars an hour. They bill for their time and that's how they make a living. What if the Care Manager bills you for just leaving a message on your phone? Some will do that. By the way, where the hell is their oversight? Who is watching them? Where is their back-up? What if they are sick, on vacation, or tied up with a client? I really just roll my eyes when I hear about an independent Care manager that also has another full-time job or part-time job. I really want to toss my cookies when I find out that they also have a position like a Discharge Planner at a hospital. Makes you wonder how they get their leads?

My point is, do your homework. Cheaper is not always less expensive. You find that out the hard way. You get what you pay for and for some people they don't have a lot of resources, but for an extra dollar or two you really have to see what it is that you are paying for. That's the part that really kills me. The people that want to save the extra money and they make arrangements with an independent contractor and then they are totally shocked when that individual steals their jewelry, medications, and takes over as durable power of attorney.

It might interest you to know about women that prey on elderly men and take them for all they are worth. You might not know this, but there are organized mafias that train and recruit individuals solely to prey on the elderly and manipulate them into signing everything over to them. I would go into greater detail, but I really value my knee caps.

I happen to live near one of the wealthiest communities in North America. You would think that there would be a plethora of business due to the financial resources. However, the wealthy like to hire their own employees. This works out just great until the employers' level of need increases to the point that they require someone that can handle personal care or has more expertise with an aging individual. It's kind of a bummer when the illegal employees that have been working for room and board and maybe a salary have to suddenly find a new home and source of employment. It's true.

Here's an interesting story. A local Trust Officer contacted my organization to conduct an assessment for their clients. The clients had made their own care giving arrangements. The clients finances were now going to be managed by a Trust Officer and they typically will not work with or make checks to independent contractors. They will, in general, require the clients to use an established agency. Our Care Manager met with the Trust Officer and she completed her detailed findings.

Our Care Manager had determined that the cost of a live-in care giver for two people that required a high level of care and Care Management oversight would probably cost around eleven thousand dollars per month. Does that seem like a lot to you? It's not really. Not in a wealthy neighborhood in California. An estate attorney will tell you that a typical range for the same level of care will probably run you between ten and twelve thousand dollars per month. What would be another option for those individuals? Probably a skilled nursing home that costs around two hundred and fifty dollars a day for a private room. You do the math and also consider if you would like a skilled nursing setting or one-on-one care in your own home.

So maybe you are a little blown away at the price tag? What is so interesting is what these people were paying on a weekly basis for the previous five years. They were paying about six thousand a week. A week! The Care Manager billed about eighty five dollars an hour for her time. However, if one of the care givers did not show up for a shift she would cover for them and charge her rate, instead of the typical care giver rate that was close to twenty something an hour. Oh, it gets better. After we had incorporated services we had to turn away the parade of vendors that would show up to the home. The vendors like the plumber. You know, the plumber that arrived when there were no plumbing issues. If not apparent to you I will just lay it out there. The Care Manager created another revenue stream for herself that involved faux repairs and was probably getting some kick back from the vendors or at least making her friends some money.

Here is the part that is really going to slay you. After we brought this to the attention of the adult children they still wanted to know if there was a way to keep the independent Care Manager as part of their parents' care plan. They said their parents really bonded with her and they didn't want to upset their parents and take her away from them. Our Care Manager and the Trust Officer highly advised against it.

I am not sure if the Trust Officer and my company would have worked with the family if they decided to stay engaged with the independent Care Manager. We certainly didn't want to be associated with someone that could be considered a financial abuser. Seriously, you have to wonder what is going through peoples' minds sometimes. I wonder if when they run out of wood for their fireplace if they just use stacks of dollar bills.

CHAPTER 19 – I WANT TO GO HOME

Everybody wants to go home. Home is where the heart is. It's not an uncommon request for an elderly person to repeatedly make the request to return home when they are in a hospital. They could be very demented and living in a memory care unit for several years and still make the request. It really pulls on the heart strings of family members. I really feel for them. It's a tough decision to place a parent, but sometimes it's the best thing to do.

Here I am working for a company that provides solutions to assist people to remain in their own homes and our Care Managers would sometimes suggest to the families that placement is their best option. There can be many reasons for that. It could be due to financial reasons, a more adaptable environment for that individual, and what about their spouse or care giver? People give up their lives to take care of others. What if there is a very healthy spouse in the home that has many good years left and they are slowly deteriorating both physically and emotionally as they try to take care of their loved one? Gives new meaning to the vow – For better or for worse.

We are all creatures of habit. Sooner or later we can get use to change in our environment and new routines. I have seen many people that were resistant to moving to a senior community, but after the while they can really bloom. You have to take into consideration the history of some of these people. Some at the age of five or less was put to work. Some times in factories. They may have had lost siblings or even their parents at young ages due to the lack of medicines and information about disease at the time. They lost their childhoods. They are well into their eighties and nineties and some will tell you that they don't even know how to have fun. They never got to play as children.

Upon a visit to a SNF or memory care unit you might see some woman holding a baby doll or a stuffed animal that is snuggled over their shoulder. You know why babies and puppies are so cute? They are biologically created that way so you will have an additional desire to care for them. However, an adult in diapers, drooling, agitated, and refusing to bathe is not so cute to many people. They don't always get the attention that they need or deserve.

There is also the emotional dynamics with family members. It's difficult for adult children to understand that the person that raised them and took care of them needs their help in the same way. For crying out loud, you don't tell your parent what to do. You respect them and all elders. The reality is that some adults start behaving like children. They require monitoring and supervision. The child becomes the parent and there is a role reversal.

There is a tremendous amount of guilt for some children. They want to respect their parents' wishes, but what the parent wants and what the parent needs are not always the same. Forget about when you put siblings and relatives that have different opinions in the mix. It becomes a real mess sometimes. Often money has an underlying influence on people's decision making process. I encourage everyone to consider in investing in an estate plan or get your advanced directives together at the minimum.

Our company helped people in uncovering their options and plans, but there are many that do not know about our kind of services. They are never given the option and your options are only as good as the information you are given sometimes. Some people that are in a hospital are transferred to a SNF. The hospital makes that recommendation and all of a sudden they are transferred to a SNF. The families aren't even aware that they have an option of what SNF they can go to.

Then there is the downright laziness and politics that go between hospitals. My buddy that works at a hospital told me of a patient that they had transferred to another hospital that was about four hours north due to the patient's medical needs. The patient became a candidate for hospice and they were declining rapidly. Ideally the patient's family wanted to return their loved one home. The originating hospital was happy to facilitate discharge plans for the family and coordinate home services for them. The hospital up north quickly arranged for a transfer back to the originating hospital which had to eat up the cost of the ambulatory ride and remaining days of the patient.

That patient could have returned home. The other hospital was lazy and the family did not know any better so they watched their loved one die in the hospital. It was due to total laziness and politics within the medical system. Those are the things that just aren't apparent to people. And why would they be apparent? How would one know? That's why you have to ask questions. You have to ask what all your options are. It's like my dad always said, "Jess, there are a few things in life you pay people a service for. Your car and taxes are two of them." Well, I can add a few more things to that list now.

You got to leave room for those kids that have poor relationships with their parents and some with good reason. Some parents have been miserable to their kids their whole lives and then those kids have to take responsibility for them. In cases where there is limited money or a refusal to spend it, the next of kin are determined as a responsible party. If an elderly person becomes harmful to themselves or others somebody has to take responsibility for them. As much as I feel bad for the elderly that have neglectful children, my heart really goes out to the abused children that are forced to take care of their parent.

I really feel for the kids that are trying to make arrangements for their parents and they are so embarrassed to share necessary details. Like the fact that their parent is totally prejudice and would not welcome a caregiver that comes from a particular ethnic background. Some children are humiliated at the condition of the house that their parent is living in and the fact that they won't put their dog to sleep that has broken hips, smells, and wears a diaper. One daughter indicated that her dad was super sweet, gets along with just about everybody, but would not tolerate a care giver that has any Republican views. I get it. My mother wouldn't either.

I really feel bad for the spouses that have to place their loved ones. It's a tough call when someone is in a SNF and the family is trying to determine if returning them home is best or if it would be a better transition to place them. The fact that they are in a SNF is traumatic enough, but returning home with a high level of acuity or advanced dementia is sometimes difficult to manage. Placing from home to a RCFE is tough as well. It's just important that when that decision is made that the loved one will be going to their best option. You don't want to have to make them move again. You want to make sure their new environment is a very comfortable setting and home.

CHAPTER 20 – GOODBYE, NORMA JEAN

I continued to visit Norma in her home at the Assisted Living Community. I remember one day she was in the dining room and at a table with three other women. I walked up to Norma and held her hands. I got her standard greeting and compliments. She was still frustrated with the fact that I had not landed a life partner.

One of the three other women said, "Who are you?"

Another woman replied, "That's her daughter."

Norma looked confused. It was just for a moment. I was about to explain to everyone that I was not Norma's daughter, but another moment passed and all was forgotten. I stayed in the dining area and helped the other employees distribute the meals. I am sure they appreciated it. They had a large group to assist.

I had become a real regular fixture in the senior care community. I was becoming what Mitch and my company was grooming me for. I was becoming an expert. Not so much an expert like a Geriatric Care Manger is but I was the one that professionals started turning to for senior care related questions. I had become a center of influence for many decision makers and referrers.

I would often aid in the marketing and education of other professionals. I would take them on visits with me to the various senior communities. I would always stop in to visit with Norma and introduce her to the professional that was accompanying me that day. Sometimes she would be in her room and be putting on her jewelry. I would look at her pictures on her dresser. There was the picture of her handsome son. There was the picture of her so happy and sitting next to her husband. I remember those pictures from the first time I ever met Norma in her home. I can still see them in my mind now.

Sometimes Norma would be sitting in her chair in the living room with the other residents and they would be listening to a live artist that would be playing a guitar or the piano. One time, I was taken back to see her sitting on the couch holding hands with a gentleman one day. That gentleman happened to be a client of ours as well. I know his wife was, but her level of need was greater at the time and she was in a more skilled setting. Well, Norma sure looked happy.

Sometimes our caregiver would take Norma for an outing and for one reason or another she would come visit our office. I would be jealous because she would be telling all the other women in my office how beautiful they were. I wanted Norma to myself and all her compliments, too. On one of her visits someone took a picture of Norma and me together. I cherish that picture.

There was a new professional, Lydia, in the community and she had not had a chance to tour the senior communities in the area. Lydia had a lot of experience with the geriatric population and people with dementia. Peggy and I spent a day with her touring different places and our last visit was at Norma's home.

I introduced Norma to Peggy and Lydia. Pegs had met her a few times. Norma and I held hands and I knelt down to talk to her for a while. Lydia, Pegs and I continued to get a tour of the individual rooms. On the way out we passed Norma in her chair. As we were getting closer Lydia said, "She is going to smile when you get closer." Norma did. She smiled and lit up when I passed her. Maybe she started to recognize me? I'll never really know.

That was the last time I saw Norma. I always wondered if I was going to have a total meltdown when she died. I used to get so sad just thinking about her not being around or what it would be like if I went by where she lived and she wasn't there. I hated how I was told about her passing. Patty, Janey and I were in our conference room together and Patty said, "Oh, Norma died a few days ago." I immediately looked at Janey who locked eyes with me. I think she thought I was going to lose it. Janey knew how I adored Norma. I probably would have lost it if Patty wasn't there. I probably would have had a meltdown and crawled into Janey's lap.

It's strange because I didn't really cry. Although, that was just due to the shock factor. A little time had passed and I found it difficult to talk about Norma. Before I would always talk about her and share my experiences of her with other professionals, but then I couldn't seem to get the words out. I would start to tear. The weird thing is I started to talk to Norma. I think in some weird way she can hear me better now. I think she is happy and is with her son and husband.

In life there are many people that will come and go. It sometimes seems that there is no rhyme or reason for the people you encounter and the experiences you share with them. However, in my heart of hearts I believe that there are absolutely are no coincidences in life. Ever. There is always a reason and lesson to be learned. Always. I also believe in my heart of hearts that as long as you keep people in your thoughts they will always be with you. I have Norma with me often.

CHAPTER 21 – LIFE GOES ON, EVEN AFTER THE THRILL OF LIVING IS GONE

When you work in an industry that has a lot of pain, suffering and death you often question what life is all about. It's hard to process sometimes what others have to go through. It's difficult to see your loved ones digress. I would think about all the cases of the abused elderly and the horror stories of these defenseless victims. And those are just the ones you know about. What about all the stories you don't know about?

You see families doing their best to support each other. You see families that try to sabotage things and tear each other apart. You are blown away at the strength and stamina of some people. Where there is life, there is hope. Hope is the last thing to go. You might have a hard time wrapping your mind around things and ask the question, "Why?" You always have to consider the answer to be, "Why not?"

I sometimes think that one of the reasons I was given the opportunity to work in this industry is to prepare me for when I have to assist my parents in their later years. I don't know how that will quite work. I can't imagine the thought of my parents not being the solid pair that they are and the major hub for the rest of the family. The thought of them being gone is unbearable to me. I imagine if my father passed away that the rest of the family would spontaneously combust. We can't possibly exist without him. I know I'll be lost the day I lose my mother. She's my best friend. She will be the first one I want to call.

This industry is also filled with love. Sometimes so much love and support that you are amazed what big hearts and energy some people have for others. There are selfless care givers and professionals that dedicate their lives on improving the lives of others around them. They sometimes give more of themselves and sacrifice their own lives in a lot of ways for the people they love. It's true that there are a lot of terrible things in the world. There are also many beautiful blessings as well.

At my age I have been around family and friends that have babies. There is a lot of preparation for a new baby in this world. They will need all those things to sustain their life. The baby needs nutrients and nurturing. They require comfort. They need to be held and touched. Holding a baby is very important. Some babies that don't get enough nurturing or touch can actually die of a broken heart.

Various beliefs or religious backgrounds can have ideas of when and where a baby originates in terms of time and space. However, I think it is pretty safe to say that before that baby arrives, they did not exist as we know them to exist. We have no past memory of their existence and yet when they arrive we love and nurture them with everything they need in order to survive and be comfortable. We offer as much love and support that we are capable to give them.

From whence we came and whence we go, is it not the same place? Why is there sometimes not as much love and support to the people in need at the end of their life? Why do we not sometimes love and comfort someone on their way out of existence with as much of the same love and respect as when they came into existence? There is also the undeniable fact that life is so precious and we never know when it will end.

That is something to reflect on. The love and compassion

we feel for new beings. What possibly happens between the time from birth to death to change anything regarding how we feel about another being other than the feelings of love and compassion? Emotional attachments and a whole other bunch of stuff. That's what happens.

"In the end these things matter most:

How well did you love?
How fully did you live?
How deeply did you let go?"
— *Gautama Buddha*